WIMBLEDON
2005

THE CHAMPIONSHIPS
WIMBLEDON
OFFICIAL ANNUAL 2005

Neil Harman

Publisher **Eddie Taylor**
Art editor **Robin Castle**
Designer **Nav Khokhar**
Production **Laura Fell**
Photo research
Getty Images, Elaine Childs
Editorial team
**Stephen Mitchell,
Elizabeth Hodgson,
Dale Harry**

This first edition
published in 2005 by
Profile Sports Media,
5th Floor, Mermaid House,
2 Puddle Dock,
London EC4V 3DS

Profile Sports Media is part
of Profile Media Group Plc

ISBN: 1 903135 48 6

Printed by Butler and Tanner

CONTENTS

FOREWORD

TIM PHILLIPS
Chairman of The All England Lawn Tennis and Croquet Club
and the Committee of Management of The Championships

EVERY YEAR WIMBLEDON GENERATES drama and stories aplenty and the 119th Championships were no exception.

Roger Federer won his third men's singles title in succession, becoming the third gentleman to win such a hat-trick since the Open Tennis era began in 1968 (Pete Sampras and Bjorn Borg also accomplished this achievement).

Our lady champion, Venus Williams, won her final against Lindsay Davenport from match point down (a feat last achieved 70 years ago by Helen Wills Moody) in the longest ladies' singles final ever played at Wimbledon, lasting two hours and 45 minutes. The title was just reward for the hard work Venus had invested in her game in an effort to emulate her Wimbledon successes of 2000 and 2001.

In the men's doubles our champions, Stephen Huss and Wesley Moodie, had to play through our qualifying competition even to secure their place in the main draw. They became the first qualifiers to win a Championship event at Wimbledon, and Wimbledon is the only Grand Slam that even holds a qualifying competition for doubles. In winning, Stephen won prize money that exceeded his career earnings till then – and this was the first main tour event they had played together. Meanwhile, Todd Woodbridge, past winner of a record nine men's doubles titles at Wimbledon, played his last match before retirement appropriately enough on Centre Court.

In the ladies' doubles, Cara Black successfully defended her title without losing a set – but this year with a new partner, Liezel Huber. On returning to the dressing room after her triumph, Cara secured another new partnership when Brett, her off-court partner, proposed to her and she accepted.

As I say, Wimbledon generates drama and stories aplenty. I very much hope that you enjoy this record of the 119th Championships held at the All England Club.

INTRODUCTION
NEIL HARMAN

A WEEK BEFORE THE OPENING OF THE 119th Championships, a Thanksgiving service was held at the Sacred Heart Church in Wimbledon for the life of Reginald Edward Hawke Hadingham. To those fortunate enough to have known him, he was always just "Buzzer".

The chairman of the All England Club from 1983 to 1989, Buzzer was credited for having given The Championships a more welcoming visage. He had gone out of his way to reach out, especially to the players, the event's lifeblood, delivering them hand-written notes, and charming them with his wit and elegance. He made them feel as if Wimbledon was really *their* Wimbledon.

It was a wonderfully spirited service, honouring Hadingham's war-time heroics, his transformation of sporting goods company Slazenger (still the only company with a logo on the court backdrops at Wimbledon), his work for charity, his remarkable poetry.

It was a gloriously sunny morning. A 20-minute journey from the church, the qualifying competition was opening at Roehampton; 128 men and women with hope in their hearts and a desire to make certain they were again one of the next 128 in the draw for The Championships proper. Vladimir Voltchkov from Belarus, the 2000 semi-finalist, was in the field, as was Arnaud Clement, the Australian Open runner-up in 2001. In the women's section was Clarisa Fernandez of Argentina, a semi-finalist at Roland Garros three years earlier. Chris Guccione of Australia defeated Olivier Patience of France 4-6, 7-6, 23-21 in the opening round, a three set match that lasted three hours and a minute. This was extraordinarily tough.

But that was how it was supposed to be. There were those, Lleyton Hewitt for one, who felt that Wimbledon had made it tougher by introducing a grass-court formula into their seeding deliberations – in which 100 per cent of a player's form on grass the previous year, and 75 per cent the year before that, was factored in. As such, Hewitt, the No.2 player in the world, found himself at No.3 in the seeds behind America's Andy Roddick. As it turned out, he would suffer the double whammy of being drawn in the same half as the defending champion Roger Federer, knowing that he would therefore meet him at the semi-final stage.

There was debate about the state of the courts and Wimbledon's decision, for the first time in ten years, to fall into line with tournaments across the world and open the cans of new tennis balls on court a few moments before they were due to be used. Tim Henman, for one, was mightily relieved at that.

The Club circulated its "Preparation of the Court for The Championships, 2005" memorandum that confirmed that, in order to improve durability, this was the fifth year that the courts had been sown with 100 per cent Perennial Ryegrass, which would strengthen the sward in order to withstand the increasing wear of the modern game. It was also noted that "there has been no intention either this year or in previous years to produce slower courts or ones suited for a particular type of game." And "unlike other surfaces, grass is a living plant in an outdoor environment and weather varies throughout the year. Weather conditions in the run up to The Championships will have some effect on the way the courts ultimately play."

Those with recent form on grass would, therefore, stand a good chance. Federer had once again won the Gerry Weber Open in Halle, Roddick secured the Queen's Club title for a third year in succession. But Henman had lost in the third round, muttering darkly about not quite knowing how he was supposed to play.

Chris Gorringe shares the moment
with champion Roger Federer

Once again, the Lawn Tennis Association chose to have a wild card play-off, which was won by the No.3 player Alex Bogdanovic, and among the Club's formal nominees were previous runner-up Mark Philippoussis of Australia, James Blake from the USA and, on the back of an inordinate amount of pre-event publicity, Andy Murray from Dunblane, the reigning US Open boys' champion, who had made such an eye-catching Davis Cup debut for Great Britain in Israel four months earlier. At Queen's, he had also come within two points of defeating Sweden's Thomas Johansson.

The only non-British wild card into the ladies' singles went to Cara Black from Zimbabwe, a two-time doubles champion in 2004. How Miss Black might fare was as difficult to conclude as how any of the ladies would. It was a fascinatingly open race. Maria Sharapova, Russia's spellbinding champion, had won Birmingham for the second successive year, Kim Clijsters triumphed at Eastbourne and Mary Pierce at Rosmalen in Holland. Justine Henin-Hardenne, the French

Open champion, had skipped the grass in order to make certain she was physically fit after so long out with a viral infection. America's Lindsay Davenport, the world No.1, had never bothered with warm up events.

But that was all premise, all surmise, all conjecture, it filled the pre-tournament pages nicely, but it meant nothing at all. Only now would we know for sure. As the first day of a new Wimbledon dawned, it was as it had been a week earlier, gloriously sunny, when we had reminisced of Buzzer Hadingham, the old chairman.

Alan Mills surveys Centre Court for the final time

I was reminded of a section of a poem he had once written in appreciation of his own father-in-law:
Do you not notice how, now he is gone,
We think of all he stood for and achieved,
To help us as each day we journey on,
Thus sharing much that he himself believed.

SO MUCH OF WIMBLEDON'S SPECIAL FEEL owes much to the steadfastness of its personnel, the knowledge that whatever happens, the system would not founder because of the quality of the people at its helm. As such, at the end of the event, two of The Championships' most loyal subjects were acclaimed on Centre Court. Before the journey's end in 2005, Christopher Gorringe, the Chief Executive of the Club for the past 26 years and Alan Mills, the Referee for the past 23, were called forward to receive a royal handshake and the warm acclaim of everyone in the stadium – particularly those behind the scenes who knew exactly the effect that Gorringe and Mills had had on so many fortnights and a lot more in between. Somehow, like the passing of a former chairman, a little of the light had gone out. ●

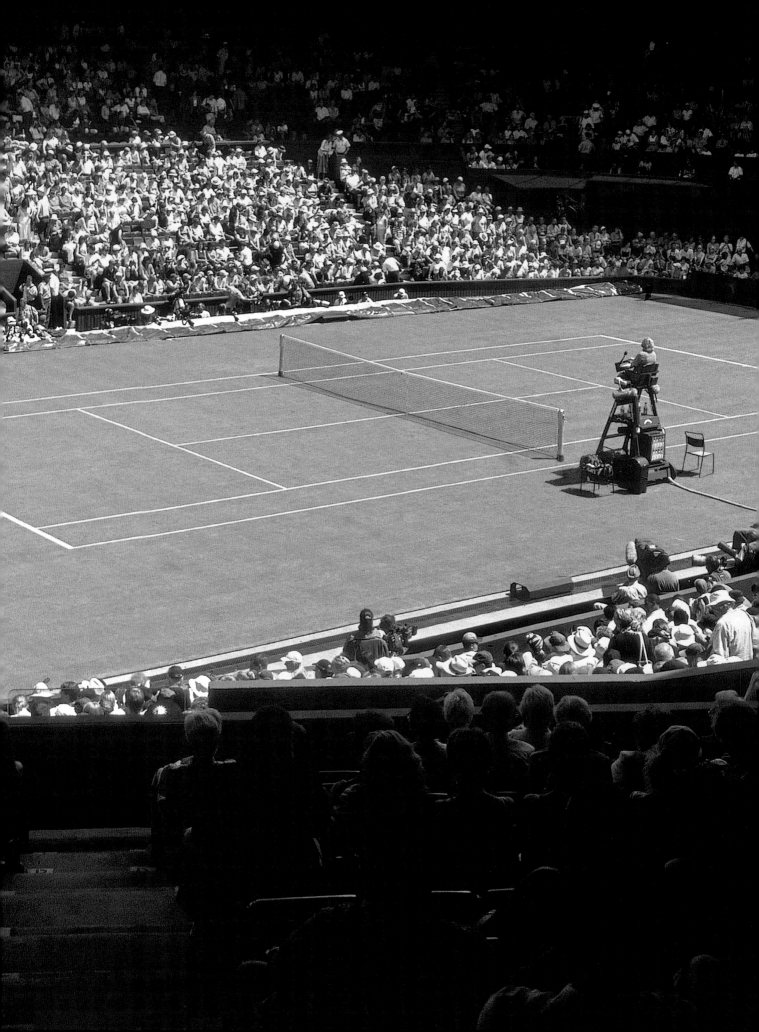

ROGER FEDERER

SEEDED 1ST

Age: 23
Born: Basel, Switzerland

Since defending his Wimbledon title successfully in 2004, the finest player in the world had clinched the US Open for the first time and retained the Masters Cup in Houston. Though he had lost in the semi-finals of the 2005 Australian Open to Marat Safin and the French Open to Rafael Nadal, Federer returned to SW19 on the back of seven tournament victories on three different surfaces and a grass court winning streak of 29 matches. Having spent the entire 2004 season on his own, he had asked Tony Roche, the former Wimbledon doubles title holder, to become his coaching consultant. Everyone accepted that it would need a dip in his form or a huge rise in someone else's for him to be troubled.

ANDY RODDICK

SEEDED 2ND

Age: 22
Born: Omaha, USA

Wimbledon's grass court seeding formula having been factored into the equation, Roddick leapt a couple of places from No.4 in the world to the second seed. He was now a three-time Stella Artois champion at the Queen's Club and was one of only four men in the field who had won three or more grass court titles, that included Federer, Lleyton Hewitt and Greg Rusedski. A semi-finalist at the Australian Open – where he lost to Hewitt – he had succumbed in the second round of the French Open to Jose Acasuso of Argentina, having led by two sets to love. He also had a new coach, Dean Goldfine, who enjoyed great success with Todd Martin.

Rafael NADAL

Age: 19
Born: Mallorca, Spain
At Roland Garros three weeks earlier, this extraordinary talent had lifted his first grand slam title just two days after his 19th birthday, having beaten Federer in the semi-final. He then said that his lifetime's ambition was to win Wimbledon. Nadal had been a revelation since the turn of the year, duelling famously with Lleyton Hewitt in the Australian Open, and leading Federer by two sets to love and 4-1 in the final of the Nasdaq-100 Open in Key Biscayne, Florida, before winning Masters Series titles in Monte Carlo and Rome, defeating Guillermo Coria of Argentina on both occasions. Much rested on whether his footwork would be as secure on grass as it had been on clay.

Lleyton HEWITT

Age: 24
Born: Adelaide, Australia
This was a seventh consecutive Wimbledon appearance for the 2002 champion, who was also the US Open champion in 2001. Australia held its breath when he reached the final in Melbourne for the first time – he lost to Marat Safin – before requiring surgery in March to remove a cyst from his right foot and then cracking two ribs in an accident at his new home in Sydney. His absence from the French Open had broken a run of 25 successive grand slam appearances. Coming into the event, he had won 24 singles titles – third in the list of active players behind Andre Agassi and Federer.

MARAT SAFIN

SEEDED 5TH

Age: 25
Born: Moscow, Russia
At long last, the former world No.1 had built on his triumph at the US Open in 2000, lifting the Australian Open in Melbourne in January, defeating Roger Federer in the semi-final and Lleyton Hewitt in a tumultuous final. He had ended last year with a marvellous run of results, posting a 24-5 autumn record, winning the indoor Masters in Madrid and Paris. He can be both temperamentally brittle but brilliant if the mood takes him, and can win a match – and lose one – at the flick of a switch. Having reached the final on the grass of Halle a week before The Championships, Safin was prepared to talk up his chances a bit more favourably. He had lost in the first round in 2004 to Dmitry Tursunov, his fellow Russian.

TIM HENMAN

SEEDED 6TH

Age: 30
Born: Oxford, England
Having complemented his French Open semi-final achievement last year by reaching the same stage of the US Open for the first time, he secured a place in the Masters Cup in Houston, also a first. Henman ended the year ranked No.6 – the fifth time in his career the British No.1 had been a top-ten player at the conclusion of a year. In 2005, however, he had not been beyond a quarter-final, losing in the third round of the Australian Open to Nikolay Davydenko of Russia, and to Luis Horna of Peru in the second round at Roland Garros. Still coached by Pete Sampras's ex, Paul Annacone, though expectations seemed high, they were not as intense as they had been in previous years.

NIKOLAY DAVYDENKO

SEEDED 8TH

Age: 24
Born: Severodonezk, Ukraine
One of the fastest improving (and fastest) players on the ATP Tour, Davydenko had begun the year ranked No.28 but had never won a round at Wimbledon in three previous attempts. Clearly he was suited to every other surface as he had reached the quarter-finals in Australia (he beat Henman in the third round, but lost to Roddick), and in Rotterdam and Dubai, before embarking on a highly successful clay court run, winning St Poelten, Austria, the week before the French Open, and reaching semi-finals in Hamburg and Barcelona, before clawing his way to the semi-finals at Roland Garros, losing in five sets to Argentine Mariano Puerta.

SEBASTIEN GROSJEAN

SEEDED 9TH

Age: 27
Born: Marseille, France
A semi-finalist in the past two Wimbledons, whose career had topped at No.4 in 2002, he was one of those players whose style allowed him to switch from surface to surface with no sense of alteration to either rhythm or tactic. One of the smoothest movers on the tour, he had a wickedly deceptive serve and a flashy forehand that worked as often as it failed him. Grosjean had profited enormously from Wimbledon's grass court formula, moving over 20 places to a prime ranking. The highlight of his year so far had been reaching the final of the clay court tournament in Houston, Texas, where he lost to Andy Roddick.

MARIA SHARAPOVA

Age: 18
Born: Nyagan, Russia
Was a wild card in 2003, when she lost in the third round; was the No.15 seed in 2004, and walked away with the title in glorious style. Sharapova was the embodiment of tennis youth – ferociously competitive, full of herself – whose only weakness was a tendency to push her forehand. This year, Sharapova had reached the quarter-final or better in all ten events played, reaching the semi-finals of the Australian Open for the first time, where she lost to eventual champion Serena Williams despite holding three match points. Her third title of the year had come at Birmingham a week before Wimbledon – a happy omen considering she had won at Edgbaston Priory in 2004 en route to the greatest day of her life.

LINDSAY DAVENPORT

SEEDED 1ST

Age: 29
Born: Palos Verdes, USA
A 15-year tour veteran, Davenport had not won a grand slam title since the 2000 Australian Open and had spoken at last year's Wimbledon about the prospect of retirement. After that, she won 17 matches in a row on hard courts entering the US Open, where she lost to Svetlana Kuznetsova in the semi-finals. Her appetite re-whetted, Davenport began 2005 by reaching the final of the Australian Open and, although she lost to Serena Williams, she became the first woman in the Open Era to win 50 singles matches in Melbourne. She reached the quarter-finals of the French Open for the first time in six years, having beaten Kim Clijsters in the fourth round, after trailing 1-6, 1-3.

AMELIE MAURESMO

SEEDED 3RD

Age: 26
Born: St Germain en Laye, France
The consummate all-court player who has the game to win but always falls short on the biggest occasions. It seemed remarkable that, given her poor grand slam record – one final appearance in Melbourne as a non-seed in 1999 – she should have reached the No.1 ranking on the WTA Tour last September. She won two titles in 2005, at Antwerp indoors and on clay in Rome. She seemed almost relieved when she lost in the third round of the French Open to Anna Ivanovic, yearning for the release of playing anywhere else but Court Central at Roland Garros. She lost in the first round of Eastbourne, so who knew what form she would be in?

SERENA WILLIAMS

SEEDED 4TH

Age: 23
Born: Saginaw, USA
The beaten finalist from 2004 had ended the year with a sixth top-ten finish but her lowest spot in six years, at No.7. Much of this had to do with the eight month lay-off recovering from knee surgery, after which she had an intermittent record, losing to her lowest ranked opponent in eight years in Linz, Austria, and to Jennifer Capriati in the quarter-finals of the US Open – a match scarred by the most controversial line-call of the year. Reached the final of the WTA championships in Los Angeles but, clearly troubled by an abdominal injury, lost to Sharapova in the final from 4-0 up in the final set. Her response was to win the Australian Open, her sixth grand slam title, in January.

Svetlana
KUZNETSOVA

SEEDED 5TH

Age: 19
Born: St Petersburg, Russia
Cemented an extraordinary year for Russian women's tennis by becoming the third successive grand slam champion following Anastasia Myskina (Paris) and Maria Sharapova (Wimbledon) by winning the US Open title in New York. Her 60 singles match wins in the year placed her third behind Lindsay Davenport and Amelie Mauresmo in 2004 successes. Kuznetsova left home in Russia for the same Sanchez/Casal Academy in Barcelona, where Scotland's Andy Murray hones his skills. A pugnacious, powerful hitter, she has a tremendous attitude towards the sport. Might have halted Justine Henin-Hardenne's progress to the French Open title had she taken two match points in the third set of their fourth round match.

Elena
DEMENTIEVA

SEEDED 6TH

Age: 23
Born: Moscow, Russia
This strikingly tall, blonde Russian had reached two grand slam finals in 2004: the French, where she lost to Anastasia Myskina, her compatriot, in two sets; and the US Open, where she suffered similarly against Svetlana Kuznetsova. Dementieva had done remarkably to reach the final at Flushing Meadows, for Jennifer Capriati, her semi-final opponent, was three times a break up and served for the match at 6-5 before losing a tight tie-break. Still coached by Olga Morozova, the 1974 finalist, there were signs that Dementieva was overcoming her serving phobia that tormented her at all the wrong moments. It appeared to be all that was stopping her from making a genuine grand slam challenge.

NADIA PETROVA

Age: 23
Born: Moscow, Russia
Remarkably, this Russian right-hander had not won a tournament on the WTA Tour, yet was on the way to completing a year as a top-ten player for the first time. Consistency was the Petrova watchword, for she had reached the semi-finals of the French Open in 2003, a performance equalled a month before The Championships, losing to Justine Henin-Hardenne, the eventual champion, in straight sets. Her best performance on grass had been to reach the fourth round twice. Her father Victor Petrov was a leading hammer thrower and her mother had been a bronze medallist at the 1976 Olympics in the 400 metres, so sporting achievement is clearly in the blood.

JUSTINE HENIN-HARDENNE

Age: 23
Born: Liege, Belgium
This fantastic Belgian athlete missed Wimbledon last year, one of a number of tournaments she had to pass on after being diagnosed with viral conditions that left her completely drained of energy. As such, her ranking fell from No.1 at the start of 2004 to No.8, a period in which she managed to haul herself to the Olympic gold medal. Missing the Australian Open, she returned to competitive tennis in Miami, then set off on a remarkable series, winning successive tournaments in Charleston, Warsaw and Berlin, turning up in Paris for the French Open and winning her fourth grand slam in a blistering finale, defeating Mary Pierce 6-1, 6-1.

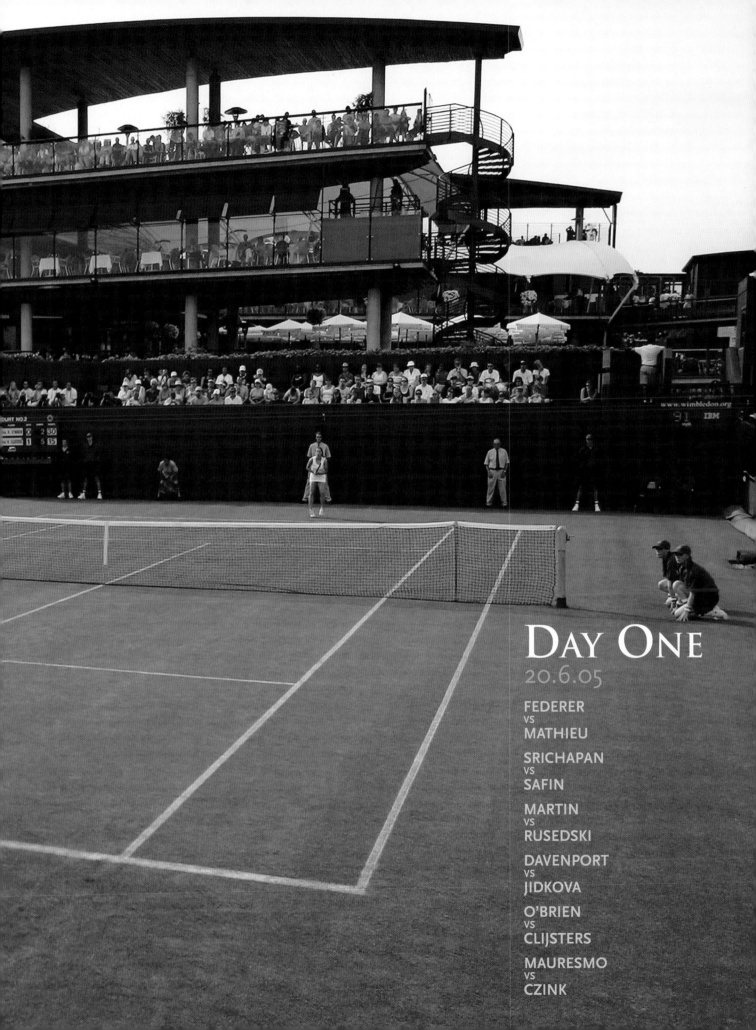

Day One
20.6.05

FEDERER
vs
MATHIEU

SRICHAPAN
vs
SAFIN

MARTIN
vs
RUSEDSKI

DAVENPORT
vs
JIDKOVA

O'BRIEN
vs
CLIJSTERS

MAURESMO
vs
CZINK

Roger Federer sails through to the second round while (left) Lindsay Davenport relishes being No.1 seed again

MONDAY, JUNE 20

LET THE GOOD TIMES ROLL. THE PULLING back of the wrought iron gates on the first day of The Championships always has a magic of its own. The place looks a picture – "how do they get their hydrangeas to look so wonderful, the grass is so green, there isn't a speck of dust or sweet wrapper anywhere." And there is obviously not an empty tin of Brasso left in SW19.

There are 256 players in the two singles draws each with a tale to tell, an ambition to fulfil; those who would relish winning a round, two would be fantasy; those who would be crestfallen not to reach the second week; those with a sneaking regard for their chances of a semi-final; and those for whom losing The Championship would be a crying shame.

Maria Sharapova would have to wait another day, the first Monday was Roger Federer's to relish. The outside courts were buzzing with activity, a couple of dreams had perished already when the side-netting at the Royal Box end was pulled apart beneath the Royal Box and Federer entered with Paul-Henri Mathieu, a young French player who had drawn the shortest straw in the sport.

"I shall be really focused walking those first few steps," Federer said, as if suggesting that he might actually stumble. "I know I'll definitely look around and say 'Wow, this is where I've had so many good moments already, but I haven't hit a ball on it since match point last year [a thunderous ace against Andy Roddick].' This is going to be

special. But the conditions are perfect, that is all I can say."

Indeed they are as there is not a mark on the courts. Only the first steps across them leave a subtle imprint. We know that by the middle of the second week the baselines will resemble a dustbowl, but on Day One, there is nothing but a sea of green. Federer is accorded a rousing welcome; what Mathieu is feeling, one can only surmise.

Actually, the Frenchman opened nervelessly on a beautiful afternoon. What a coup for him, a fellow 23-year-old ranked 58 in the world, who once cried his eyes out when he lost a two-set lead in the final rubber of a Davis Cup Final

for his country in Paris, to take an uncharted step. He had nothing to lose, nothing to hold back for but he was not going to take too much of the initiative, he would wait and see. It wasn't until five minutes had passed that the first volley – by Mathieu – was attempted and failed. "I wanted to get my rhythm first," Federer said. It came to him slowly.

Mathieu did his best, he played quality tennis but Federer had a distinct edge, and won 6-4, 6-2, 6-4. The only real alarm came when, midway through the final set, one of the ball boys at the roller end, who had been standing in the full glare of the sun, collapsed and had to be helped from the court. His replacement ▶

appeared in a flash, such is the precision with which Wimbledon does these things.

The women's world No.1 and 1999 champion Lindsay Davenport was next through the curtains, against Alina Jidkova, one of 25 Russian women in all competitions. The first set disappeared in a flash, Jidkova winning nine points, Davenport completing a rout with three consecutive aces. There was a broad smile on Jidkova's face when she won the first game of the second set, an even broader one when Davenport completed a ferocious 6-0, 6-2 victory in a manner of uncomplicated certainty.

A flame of red from the county of the white rose was the most vivid of illuminations on the opening day. David Sherwood might have struggled to continue a whole lot further on an un-Sheffield like scorcher of an

afternoon, but the manner in which he held both game and nerve together was one ray of sunshine that had not been in the forecast.

Sherwood, the 25-year-old son of Olympian parents, won a match in the main draw for the first time, defeating Ricardo Mello of Brazil, 6-4, 6-4, 6-4. For a start, he raised himself to defeat a player 206 places ahead of him in the Indesit ATP rankings, which was some feat considering he had spent the previous week struggling to get to his feet at all, after being stricken with tonsilitis. The release of his emotions when, having double-faulted away his first match point, he steered a confident volley onto the back of the baseline from where Mello was unable to lift it over the net, was manifestly understandable.

The All England Club's decision to award the lion's share of its eight wild ▶

Kim Clijsters hits a
forehand down the line.

Left: David Sherwood
soaks up the
atmosphere of his
first Wimbledon win

David Sherwood
replenishes his fluids
between games

cards to British players has long polarised opinions in the debating chambers of the sport. On one hand, the financial advantages of a couple of wins and the ranking points accrued can sustain a player through another year of making career ends meet; the counter argument is that a free pass into the world's most favoured tournament should not be granted simply because you have done something that catches authority's eye or are a favoured son. Thus, the decision to make the wild cards harder to come by based on a stricter selection process allied to ranking improvement, has been roundly welcomed.

There was no doubting the validity of Sherwood's case. Once considered too much of a lad for the LTA's liking, he poured heart and soul into winning the doubles with Andy Murray in his Davis Cup debut in Israel in March, and had risen over 300 places on the computer since the start of last year. The Centre Court might be a world away yet, but Sherwood was more than worthy of the acclaim that greeted a first round victory that, with the guarantee of at least 35 ranking points, will send him over his career-best ranking of 257.

Watching, as ever, were John and Sheila, his parents, who have rarely let their son out of sight when he has played in this country, be it in the County Cup for Yorkshire or trekking the Futures and Challengers circuits, from where

he wants a release one day. Indeed, Sherwood doesn't drive, so Mum and Dad have not only been chief supporters but chauffeurs as well. They were there, beside themselves beside Court No.6, trying to remain as detached as possible.

Mr and Mrs Sherwood don't argue that often, but they did beg to differ on how much weight David had lost during his time out with tonsilitis. "A stone," Sheila said. "Half a stone," John responded. But what they agreed was that their son, who lost in the 1998 boys' quarter-finals to Federer, thoroughly merited his place in the second round against Feliciano Lopez, the powerfully-built left hander from Spain. ▶

2004 Boys Champion Gael Monfils (above) sees off Noam Okun in the first round while Paradorn Srichaphan (below) bows his head after losing to Marat Safin

SHOCK
OF THE DAY

MARIANO PUERTA v LARS BURGSMUELLER

Well, maybe not so much of a shock, all things being considered. Puerta (right), the stocky Argentine, had reached the final of the French Open a month before – losing a match of relentlessly grinding rallies and brilliant stroke-play to Spain's Rafael Nadal – he had flown to London the following day and withdrawn from the Queen's Club event with a groin injury. Very little had been expected of the 16th seed but with Argentina playing a Davis Cup tie in Australia on grass in July, the captain was looking for his players to react positively to the surface. Puerta lost 6-1, 6-1, 6-4 and was flying home that night.

TAYLOR DENT
v DICK NORMAN

Taylor Dent (pictured), a player who had been on the wrong end of several injury concerns, had come badly unstuck against Scotland's Andy Murray at Queen's Club but was seeded No.24 given his grass court pedigree, which includes a semi-final place at the Nottingham Open in 2004. Dick Norman, a 6 foot 8 inch left hander from Waregem in Belgium, who reached the fourth round of Wimbledon a decade ago, had, at the age of 34, successfully qualified for The Championships. The fourth set tie-breaker was the crux of a serve-dominated match, Norman saving three match points – something he described as "pretty stressful as there was so much intensity on every point." Having done all he could to stay with Dent, the freckle-faced Norman inevitably relaxed at the start of the final set, not making a single first serve and double faulting twice to hand the initiative straight back. The free-swinging, net-rushing American steadied to win 7-6, 7-6, 4-6, 6-7, 6-1.

Greg Rusedski seals an
opening day win over
Alberto Martin (below)

"He has never played better," said John, bronze medallist in the 1968 400-metres hurdles in Mexico City, and he has seen most of them. Sherwood had only trained properly for two days before seeking to go out and justify the wild card that was his from the moment he and Murray joined forces to such exception in Tel Aviv. The conditions were not exactly the best for someone of a freckly complexion – Sherwood

could not decide whether to play in a hat or out of one and the red blemish across the back of his neck suggested he should have protected himself a little better.

Greg Rusedski, now the father figure in Davis Cup terms after Tim Henman's retirement from the competition was confirmed in January, opened his 13th consecutive Wimbledon campaign with a 6-3, 4-6, 6-2, 6-1 victory over Alberto Martin, who had only won four times on grass in six visits. For the grass court season, Rusedski was being coached by Martin Bohm, a Swede who had made such an impression since joining the LTA's backroom staff. The message from Bohm was: "Start aggressively, stay aggressive and finish with as much aggression as you can muster."

Rusedski recalled his first match on Court No.2, 12 years earlier. "I lost 7-6, 6-7, 7-6, 6-4 to [Stefan] Edberg. There was one break, it was lightning fast. There's no question, it's totally different now to what it was then. The grass is thicker and the balls are heavier."

It was one of a handful of complaints as Wimbledon dawned again and everything seemed utterly well with the world. ●

QUOTE
OF THE DAY

Taylor Dent on why he doesn't have time for second opinions:
"If they're going to say: 'Oh jump off the Empire State Building, you'll be fine', I'll say 'but gravity is going to happen and it's a hard floor down there, what about that?' And they say 'no, no, jump, you'll be fine'. You know, forgive me if I don't jump. That sort of thing."

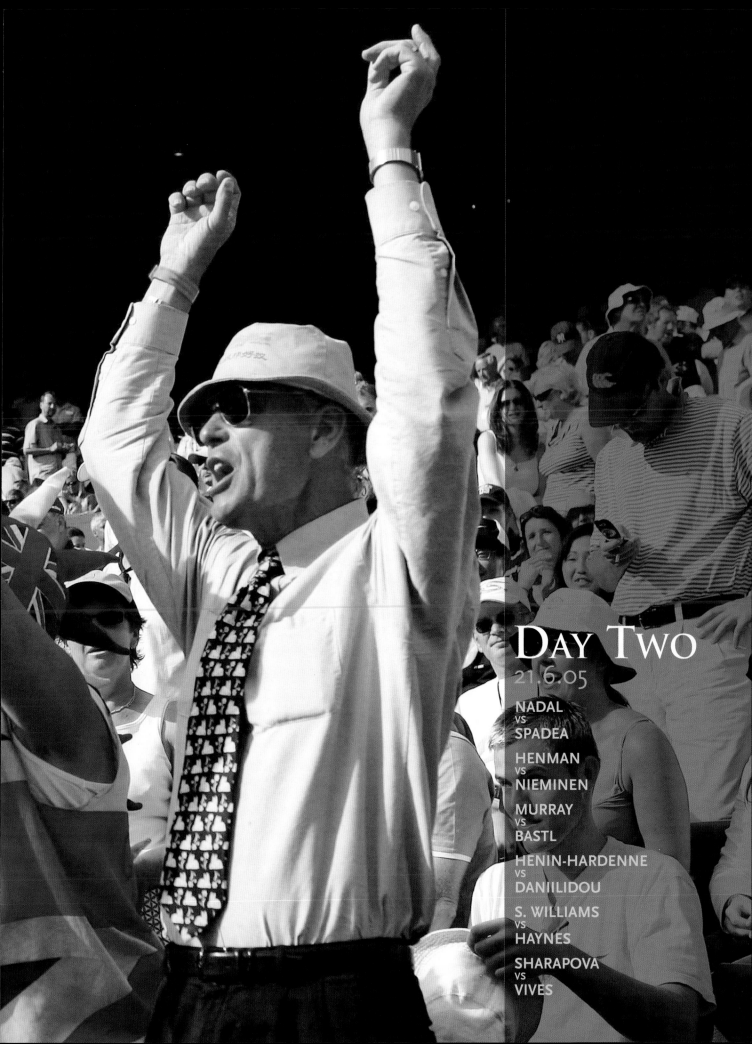

DAY TWO
21.6.05

NADAL
vs
SPADEA

HENMAN
vs
NIEMINEN

MURRAY
vs
BASTL

HENIN-HARDENNE
vs
DANIILIDOU

S. WILLIAMS
vs
HAYNES

SHARAPOVA
vs
VIVES

TUESDAY,
JUNE 21

BY A QUIRK OF THE DRAW, THE SECOND DAY happened to coincide with the launching of the Wimbledon aspirations of both the French Open champions: Belgian Justine Henin-Hardenne and Rafael Nadal, the Spaniard who had roared his way to the title in Paris two days after his 19th birthday and sparked a frenzy of tennis interest in his nation that had barely been seen before. The whole country was Rafa bananas.

Nadal, a charming boy, had made it plain in a conversation with me in Key Biscayne, Florida, in March that winning Wimbledon was at the apex of his ambition. He did not see a reason why the courts that had slowed down over the years would not suit his buccaneering style, as the bounces became truer, so he would come more into his own, able

to unleash the full ferocity of his groundstrokes. "One day, I really believe I will win Wimbledon," he said.

Henin-Hardenne had been a beaten finalist in 2001, when Venus Williams successfully defended her title, but the pugnacity and willpower of the Belgian had been demonstrated through a clay court season, both in the USA and Europe, in which she won four successive titles, rounded off with a terrible thrashing of Mary Pierce in the women's final at Roland Garros.

The first task for Henin-Hardenne was difficult, for Eleni Daniilidou, born in Hania, Crete, ranked No.73, and who had reached the fourth round in 2002, was a mighty striker of the ball and did not lack for self-belief. What happened on Court No.1 was a demoralising

moment for the Belgians who had followed Justine here in the hope she might pick up on grass where she had left off on red clay. Instead, Daniilidou caused an enormous upset, winning 7-6, 2-6, 7-5, showing remarkable composure in the latter stages as the former world No.1 did all she could to stay in the race.

How could things have turned so sour from such intense expectations? "Because I get very frustrated very quickly on grass because the bounces are never the same and I need to be patient, I need to stay very calm," Henin-Hardenne said. "For sure, for my personality it's much harder because here, everything is in two or three shots. On clay, I like it because I have the time to organise my game. I hope in the next few years I can get a better preparation." ▶

Henman scrapes through against Jarkko Nieminen

Andy Murray dons the
Henman mantle – fist
pump included

Justine Henin-Hardenne crashes out in the first round to Eleni Daniilidou

Below: The crowd take to their feet for Tim Henman

Henin-Hardenne had had to take time off after Paris to make certain the debilitating effects of the virus she had suffered during the latter stages of last year would not return. Eastbourne was by-passed, much to her regret. "Even today I can say I took the good decision because my health is my biggest concern right now," she said. "So even if I lost in the first round here, I think I took the right decision."

For Daniilidou, all was rosy. Not until after her victory did she come to realise exactly how many residents of Greece had been following her progress. "I had a tonne of SMS [texts] and phone calls after the match," she said. "So many people were following on the Internet and on the TV. It's a great feeling to know so many people care about me. Actually, tennis is not really famous in Greece. It got famous a little bit more after the Olympics, because they made new clubs, new tennis courts."

Nadal had the better end of the French Open champion's deal. Invited on to Centre Court, the first time we had seen the all-white version of his "piratas", the below the knee length trousers that were even being worn by certain members of the British press (who should know better), Nadal did not disappoint, ripping through Vince Spadea of the States, 6-4, 6-3, 6-0.

"I can play good on grass and that is not only important for today but for the next years as well, I think," he said. "I want to improve my game so I can play well in a year here."

Across on Court No.2, a player Nadal crossed swords with in the juniors was getting his first taste of the Wimbledon experience and, boy, did it taste good. "You're going to be a legend, you know that," an unbashful young lad said as he thrust an autograph book at Andy Murray, from Dunblane, Scotland. What the little fellow would have made of Tim ▶

Henman on a day when it looked as if the torch of British tennis ambition might have been passed from England to Scotland, heaven alone knew.

Henman's own legend was extended on Centre Court as he recovered from two sets down for the first time in his 12th Wimbledon to beat Jarkko Nieminen of Finland 3-6, 6-7, 6-4, 7-5, 6-2. Only in the fifth set did he play to a standard anywhere near his rank in the game; for the rest of the afternoon, it was tennis that Henman in the most capricious of moods has defined as an art form unique to him.

Goran Ivanisevic, the 2001 champion, used to talk of there being three Gorans; the good guy, the bad guy and the one who intervened in their prolonged disputes. There are two Tims; Tim the terrible and Tim the tumultuous. For two sets, terrible had the upper hand, throttling his ambitions like a hand on his windpipe, before tumultuous began to probe at the back of his mind and finally, gloriously, decorously, to the amazement of everyone and no one, finally flowered.

As unfathomable as the way the British No.1 played in the first two sets, dumping volleys, slashing at groundstrokes, unable to move his feet, the turnaround was equally improbable. Nieminen's level remained very much the same, he did not make many errors, his double-fisted backhand contrived improbable winners, he stayed mentally strong, he did what a No.70 in the world would do most days of the week. It was Henman's match to win, and his to lose. Winning only just won out.

"I just struggled with my form and that's the issue," he said. "The courts

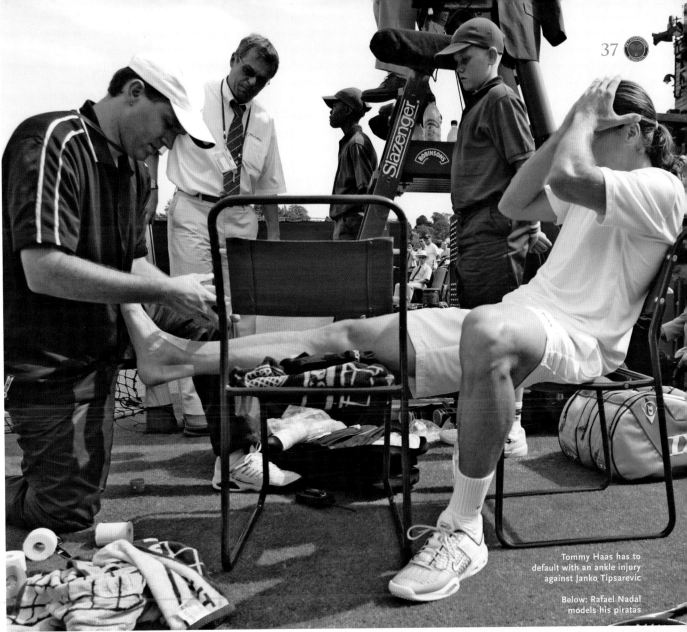

Tommy Haas has to default with an ankle injury against Janko Tipsarevic

Below: Rafael Nadal models his piratas

have changed so much here over the years, it's heavy, and slow, the ball doesn't come through, but it is the same for everyone. But I was flat with my attitude and body language and at two sets down you've got to dig in and play with what you've got. I just have to find a way to perform better, that's the challenge."

Of that there can be no doubt. What must have been whirling through his mind when he slumped into his chair having lost the second set tie-break, what Paul Annacone, his coach must have been feeling, what must his family have been going through? His mother-in-law was handing out the wine gums, but their flavour must have been perishing in his relatives' mouths.

A first round defeat, his first since 1994 when a raw teenager, would have stuck in the craw, it would have inspired crazed stories about his lack of a future, that the magic had gone, that he was a spent force. In truth, he looked all of those things after a sorry hour when he looked down at the grass and must have had trouble recognising its colour, its texture, its very aroma. And this is supposed to be his home.

He had countenanced caution because his form coming into The Championships was patchy, he did not know exactly how he should play and when he tossed away a 40-0 lead on his own serve at 3-5 in the first set to a clutch of airy-fairy shots, a pall descended. He broke in the first game of the second set but lost serve to love in the sixth game, led 4-2 in the tie-break but surrendered that when a stumbling sliced backhand service return on a Finnish second serve slid into the net.

SERENA WILLIAMS
V ANGELA HAYNES

Angela Haynes' elder brother Dontia used to play against Serena in the same public park in California. "She didn't want to lose those matches, she was always very competitive." And what about now?

"The same thing," Haynes said. It was a gripping first round match on Court No.2 as the left-handed Haynes, giving everything she had on her first appearance in The Championships, won a remarkable first set tie-break 14-12, and was serving for 5-5 in the second when the former champion suddenly found an extra gear. "I really don't know what would have happened to my career if I'd won the match," said Haynes, who came perilously close to exactly that and found that there is nothing more a Wimbledon crowd likes to see than a great player being given an extremely nasty scare. Williams eventually won 6-7, 6-4, 6-2.

Eleni Daniilidou enjoys the shade during her victory over Justine Henin-Hardenne

The third and fourth sets were each clinched on timely breaks, in the tenth game of the third and the 12th game of the fourth. Centre Court discovered its patriotic voice. Henman was flowing now, digging deep, making fantastic "gets" at the net where previously he had been all limp insecurity. It was, perhaps, typical of his day that he should reach his first match point with a remarkable, stooping backhand crosscourt volley from a fierce Nieminen attempted pass, only to toss it away with a woeful backhand service return. How could the same man play two such ridiculous shots in succession? But that is the essence of Henman.

Andy Murray, on the other hand, was in firm control of his match against George Bastl of Switzerland from the outset. On Court No.2 in 2002, Bastl had achieved the near-impossible and defeated Pete Sampras, a result from which the finest grass court player of his era would never recover. Murray cared not a jot for such history. He won 6-4, 6-2, 6-2 in thrilling fashion and, as he signed autograph after autograph, pausing to give the entering Venus Williams, a "what are you doing walking out before I've left" kind of look, you had the feeling he might indeed be a bit of a legend one day. ●

QUOTE OF THE DAY

Tim Henman after his nervy five set victory over Finland's Jarkko Nieminen:

Q: *Your family were put through the mill tonight...*
A: *Is that anything unusual?*
Q: *Looked a bit agitated tonight.*
A: *Who?*
Q: *Your whole family.*
A: *They looked agitated?*
Q: *Yes.*
A: *You must have been looking at the wrong people.*

Day Three

22.6.05

PHILIPPOUSSIS
VS
SAFIN

JOHANSSON
VS
RUSEDSKI

MIRZA
VS
KUZNETSOVA

Marat Safin falls in love with Wimbledon. For now

WEDNESDAY, JUNE 22

TO THOSE WHO HAD NOTHING BUT THE utmost admiration for Marat Safin, his talents, his manner and, yes, even his eccentricities, the idea that he might seriously believe in himself as a potential Wimbledon challenger had been too long in forming.

Safin doused such idealistic nonsense, either by showing up, shrugging his shoulders and departing very swiftly or simply not showing up at all. On the night of his defeat to Tommy Robredo of Spain in the French Open a month earlier, the annual Paris dinner that Ion Tiriac, the Romanian, and

British tennis writers throw for each other – his treat one year, ours the next – was scheduled. Tiriac still had a vested interest in Safin's career and Gerard Tsobanian, his personal manager, was in the company. I sat next to Tsobanian and it was all he could do to contain his temper at Safin's performance earlier in the day. Fortunately it did not ruin the ribaldry of the night.

Safin went from Paris to the grass of Halle, where he reached the final and there gave Roger Federer a real run for his money. In the first round of Wimbledon he had defeated the Thai,

Paradorn Srichaphan, albeit in a terrible form drought. "I wish I could have these kind of matches every day, I wish I could play the same level every day," Safin said. Tiriac and Tsobanian would have agreed.

Facing the 2003 runner-up, Mark Philippoussis, in the next round, he would need to discover that level once more, even though the Australian seemed injury prone.

The ovation Safin received after his 7-6, 7-6, 6-4 victory over Philippoussis wrapped him in a tender embrace, and acceptance in such euphoric tones from a Centre Court crowd was a symphony he never thought he would hear. The Russian had wowed them in New York and Melbourne, he had been the butt of Parisien dismay but in London, there had been muted regard for his talents.

He did not much mind because he had never really had a feel for Wimbledon in the manner of so many for whom success there is the sporting ultimate. The No.5 seed from Moscow was asked a very straightforward question after his victory – "is this the first time you've enjoyed yourself here?" He answered, just as straightforwardly: "Yup."

The rest had better watch out, for Safin and fun is a potentially lethal cocktail. He may not look as if he's

Sania Mirza during her momentous, if ultimately unsuccessful, tussle with Svetlana Kuznetsova

Lleyton Hewitt pounds
another backhand

Mark Philippoussis feels
the full force of Marat
Safin's grass revival

telling himself funny jokes, he does not
whip a whoopee cushion out and place it
on his chair at changeovers, there are no
outward signs of rib-tickling enjoyment,
but he is playing with a sense of inner
freedom. It spells fascination. It is an
integral part of his charm.

The fact that he has more talent in
his little finger than most who have ever
wielded a racket for payment, makes
him an exasperation in ever changing
hairstyles. He had chosen D'Artagnan
for Wimbledon; a moustache and
whippy goatee under a dazzle of curls,
so that he was short only of cape and foil
to complete the image. When he is at his
best, Safin can zig-zag an opponent to
pieces, cutting the ground from beneath
them and slicing through their defences.

Against the brute force of
a Philippoussis serve, he had to wait for
his moment and not get too distressed.
He actually trailed 0-40 at 4-5 down in
the first set and, if he had been in one
of his really bad moods, he would not
have dragged his way back. He trailed
in both tie-breaks but would not be
denied and finally, in the seventh game
of the third, he broke Philippoussis for
the first time with a couple of crunching
backhand passing shots. And he found it

highly amusing when the net collapsed
of its own volition.

Safin has reached the semi-finals or
better of the other three grand slams,
whereas his previous best at Wimbledon
was a quarter-final in 2001, when he lost
in four sets to Goran Ivanisevic, the
eventual champion. He wonders why he
came back at all after losing in the first
round in 1998, when he received a wild
card – though no one can quite remember
why. "I lost to [Andrei] Medvedev. No
chance. '99? Why did I play at all?

"I pass through difficult moments in
my life, really difficult times on grass for
seven years. I was never comfortable
on the surface until I played Halle
[the Gerry Weber Open in Germany]
last week. I lost to Federer in the final,
I really played some great tennis. I had
nothing to complain about. There are
a lot of things in life we don't know
exactly why they happen."

The favourites also had a reasonably
trouble free passage, Federer defeating
Ivo Minar of the Czech Republic and
Lleyton Hewitt, forced to work a deal
harder to defeat another Czech, Jan
Hernych, in four.

For Greg Rusedski, it all came to
a despairing end. There was not to be ▶

QUOTE OF THE DAY

Justin Gimelstob:
*"I was sitting watching
Corina [Morariu] and Lindsay
[Davenport] in the doubles
yesterday and there were three
guys looking up at Henman's
score and just blasting him to
shreds saying: 'I don't know why
he doesn't retire, he's never going
to win Wimbledon'. After five
minutes of this – albeit I'm
trying to lead a kinder, gentler
life – I finally snapped and said
to these guys, you know, you're
the biggest idiots I've ever come
across in my life. You guys have
an unbelieveable ambassdor for
England, he conducts himself
unbelievably well, he deals with
pressure, he's a great person,
family man, competes great,
he's had a great career. Since
when is the barometer of success
or failure being the absolute
greatest at something. I mean,
seriously, I think maybe the bar
is set too high."*

Left: Greg Rusedski
never threw in the towel
against Johansson

JOACHIM JOHANSSON
V GREG RUSEDSKI

The tie-break in the first set contained enough drama for
a whole series of *Midsomer Murders* and took up almost an entire
page of one's notebook to cover. Six of the first 11 points went
against the serve but, once the set points – two to Rusedski and
Johansson's first four – began to stack up, the server held
decisive sway. Rusedski saved Johansson's fourth with an
ace, but then the Swede picked out a fabulous backhand drive
winner and ended the 22-point marathon with an ace of his own.
Rusedski broke twice to land the second set, Johansson needed
a single opportunity to move ahead in the third. It had begun
to get extremely dark, Johansson complaining to the umpire that
"it's hard to see the ball," but they were told to complete the set
by Alan Mills, the referee, and that Johansson did, taking the
tie-break 7-5 and the match 7-6, 3-6, 6-4, 7-6.

the reprieve of a final set, a possible
stay of execution, a belated lifeline.
In the semi-darkness of what had been
a glorious summer's day, Rusedski
disappeared from Centre Court's
squinting view and there was a terribly
nagging sense at the back of one's mind
that he might not re-appear.

Over the course of 13 seasons, he had
played more grass court tennis than any
other man in the field, he lived for the
hope that he might be crowned the
champion one clear day. All through this
year, he had been plagued with difficult
draws. It was as if the tennis gods were
not in a benevolent mood, they did not
react to his consistently perky visage.
Joachim Johansson, a Swedish totem

pole – Stefan Edberg plus a few more inches – was just too tall and strong, winning 7-6, 3-6, 6-4, 7-6.

No one doubted that Rusedski had given his all, for he has never been a quitter, never offered less than his body would allow; but now, nearing 32, time and very much fitter men are accelerating away from him. Johansson is indubitably one of those, for if Rusedski served hard, he served a little bit harder, if the left hander struck it off the ground with venom, it came back from the right hand with a bit more on it. In the crunch-crunch-crunch of grass court tennis, Johansson had a bit more bite.

There were some quite remarkable statistics. Rusedski made 99 per cent of

his volleys; they were true and secure, whether from waist high or down at his toes. When his first serve landed in the box, he won 83 per cent of the points, but he landed only half as many winners and could not quite match Johansson in the ace department. As the fourth set tie-break neared its conclusion, three of the Swede's last four service points were aces. It was massive stuff from the 11th seed.

"It's disappointing when you give everything you've got, you play so well and the crowd is so much behind you," he said. I was just hoping I could have gone into a fifth set and started again tomorrow. Even on match point, I played a good point and hit a good forehand as ▶

Fans were invited to add their art to the mural that celebrates 70 years of Robinson's on Centre Court

Left: Kuznetsova finally overcomes her Indian challenger, Mirza

Right: Martina Navratilova and Anna-Lena Groenefeld size up their next victims

Below: Roger Federer receives his adoring public

well. It is a long time since I've played as well as that at Wimbledon, maybe in 2002 when I played [Andy] Roddick on Centre. The last couple of years, I haven't had the best preparation."

The reason Rusedski's entry onto Centre Court had been so late was because an Indian player named Sania Mirza had performed with memorable poise on her debut. So much so that she had significantly delayed the progress of Svetlana Kuznetsova, the US Open champion, who was only able to confirm her place in the third round after more than two hours on court.

Mirza had first come to international attention this year when she played with equal lack of inferiority against Serena Williams at the Vodafone Arena in Melbourne. Promptly, she went home to Hyderabad and caused a minor tremor in the region by winning her first Sony Ericsson WTA Tour title in her own backyard.

We could well understand why, watching her duel so fabulously with Kuznetsova before the Russian triumphed 6-4, 6-7, 6-4. Mirza said: "I love playing with the crowd, I love playing for the crowd, I loved every

second I was out there. I wanted to get the feel of every second, every ball I was hitting. I was enjoying everything out there.

"Last night, before sleeping, I was just thinking that I'm on Centre Court – I knew I was going to be on a show court, I really didn't think it was going to be Centre. I wasn't scared of who I was playing or what I was playing. I was just scared that I was playing on Centre in Wimbledon, second round."

She had no reason to be scared. She would be back. The Centre Court demanded it. ●

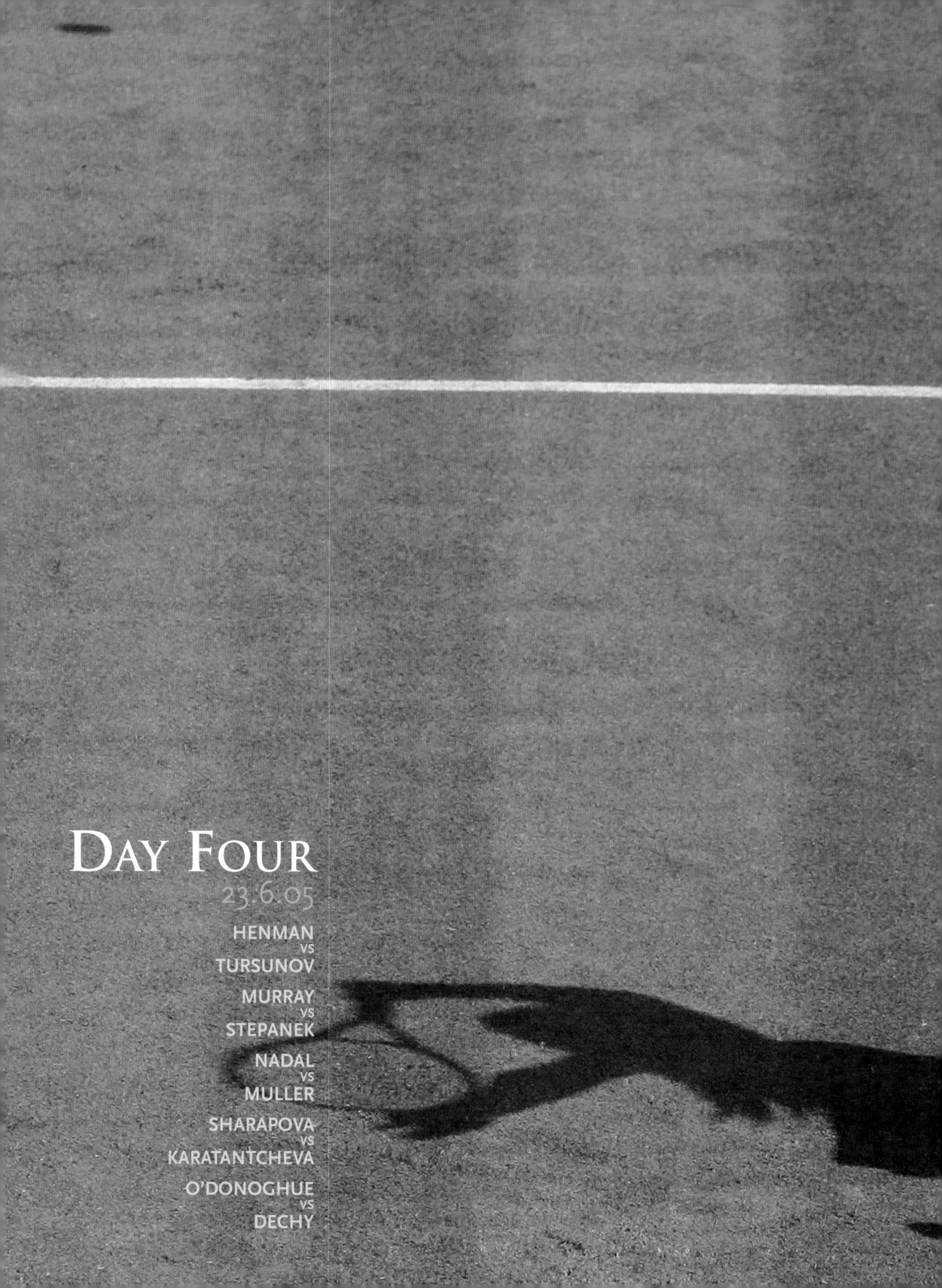

DAY FOUR

23.6.05

HENMAN
vs
TURSUNOV

MURRAY
vs
STEPANEK

NADAL
vs
MULLER

SHARAPOVA
vs
KARATANTCHEVA

O'DONOGHUE
vs
DECHY

Henman's conqueror
Dmitry Tursunov silences
the home crowd

Jane O'Donoghue was the last British competitor in the ladies' singles

THURSDAY, JUNE 23

To say that it all happened on the fourth day of The Championships did Thursday, June 23 a teensy-weensy bit of a disservice. But happen it did, non-stop, at breakneck speed, like one of those television pieces where they condense a day's movement at a sporting venue into a 30-second featurette and everyone looks like characters from a Lowry painting on speed. You needed eyes in the back of your head – and a hundred heads.

Most significantly, in a ceremony invisible to the naked eye, a torch was passed from tremulous English hands to strong and secure Scottish ones. Within two hours, across a couple of hundred yards of prime tennis green, Tim Henman lost, Andy Murray won, Wimbledon spun on its axis and, as the bottom dropped out of one world, another whirled into a new orbit.

Henman's five-set loss to Dmitry Tursunov of Russia, 3-6, 6-2, 3-6, 6-3, 6-3, coupled with Murray's 6-4, 6-4, 6-4 victory over Radek Stepanek of the Czech Republic, the 14th seed, meant that for the first time in a decade, the present British No.1 was not the last man from these islands still standing. Henman lost in the second round in 1995, Greg Rusedski went on to reach the last 16 before losing to Pete Sampras.

Now, the event was Murray's; full on, no holds barred, a single spotlight. That he could live with it there was no doubt, for this was a boy born to achieve and these are the courts that, fairly or unfairly, have made and broken the British down the years. Murray was surely not for breaking. He had won two matches in his first Championship in straight sets, and if he were to fall in the third, there would not be a shred of shame or dishonour.

Murray treated Stepanek – coached by Tony Pickard the former British Davis Cup captain, who must have wished he was 20 years younger and available on a full-time basis for Murray to give him a call – with a disdain that was remarkable. "He tried to put me off and make me ▶

The king is dead, long live the king. Andrew Murray wins his first two Wimbeldon matches without dropping a set. Henman (right) ponders his second-round loss

nervous but he ended up looking stupid," Murray said. "I knew Tim had lost, I wanted to keep the British going because they [the media] would have really hassled me if I'd lost."

But we would not. We would not have needed to. Murray's performance was one of wonderful control, of himself and his racket. He returned Stepanek's serve out of his socks, he sliced and diced from the back of the court, he moved smoothly, he did not let net-cords on match point unnerve him, he rallied more securely, served better and obdurately refused to be shaken from his iron resolve.

Compare and contrast with Henman. Yes, a wonderful player who has been in the top ten for more years than anyone, bar Andre Agassi, still wielding a racket. Yes, the best we have had on this island for decades. Yes, so close to reaching a Wimbledon final. But to lose in the second round to Dmitry Tursunov – a Russian with a bad back – a couple of days after he should have lost in the first to Jarkko Nieminen – a Finn on his honeymoon – brought with it a single, sad conclusion. That Henman's chance on grass had gone.

He had said that he has only played one decent game on the surface in four years and in the space of the last three days, he has played two extremely indifferent ones. "I will keep trying, because you know what? I love what I do," Henman said. And yet, in the first ten minutes of the match, defeat looked extremely unlikely as Henman, aware that he had begun poorly against Nieminen, came out in a blaze of aggression and intent.

Tursunov was troubled during every service game and the set was Henman's in a shade over 44 minutes. Henman ▶

had two chances to lead 2-0 in the second, could not take them and when he was broken in the third game, had three opportunities to nip the Russian renaissance in the bud. But Tursunov steadied, took the set and battle was joined. A flurry of service breaks midway through the third went Henman's way but he dropped serve in the fourth game of the fourth and, though he had two chances to break back, Tursunov produced successive aces of penetration and placement to stand firm.

When Tursunov served for the match for the second time, he struck a second service winner, drew a netted forehand

return from another second serve and another error from a backhand return. The Russian pushed one forehand into the net to give the home crowd a glimmer, only for it to be dashed by his 17th ace. "When you break down the nuts and bolts of the match, it came down to important points, 17 break points that went begging," Henman reflected. "On 15 of those I couldn't get the ball back in play. You know why? The guy was hitting aces or hitting the lines. I sit here feeling numb but what can I do about that?"

Learn to love grass again might be the answer. Much like Rafael Nadal. When

the young Spaniard lost in the second round to Gilles Muller of Luxembourg 6-4, 4-6, 6-3, 6-4, he said that he was going to have a grass court built at his club in Majorca – "because my goal until the end of my career is to win this title."

Muller had all the right strokes and played most of them at exactly the right time. A tall man, 6 foot 3 inches, and a left hander, he could use his weapons to great advantage against Nadal who, on grass, was a relative novice. "I played him on clay this year and lost 6-0, 6-2," Muller recalled, "but if you are serving well and coming to the net a lot, it is tough for the real clay courters to play well on this surface. But they are better than before, that's for sure."

The British challenge in the men's singles was reduced to a solitary competitor, and come the end of Thursday, Murray was the last person standing of either sex. Jane O'Donoghue, from Wigan, had been the one survivor from the first round but she found Nathalie Dechy, the Australian Open semi-finalist, much too experienced.

Points come and go so quickly on grass and so when O'Donoghue had a couple of sneaky looks at the French girl's first game on serve and failed to ▶

A brief moment of joy for
Rafael Nadal in his loss to
Luxembourg's Gilles Muller.
Below left: Mary Pierce shelters
from un-Londonlike heat

Maria Sharapova powers past Sesil
Karatantcheva in the second round

SHOCK
OF THE DAY

GILLES MULLER
V RAFAEL NADAL

When Great Britain won a Davis Cup
tie in Luxembourg last year and Gilles
Muller, who had defeated Arvind
Parmar in the first singles, lost to Tim
Henman in the first reverse rubber,
one of the British journalists present
predicted that the tall left-hander
would not be heard of again. It is as
well he had not passed such feelings
on to the French Open champion, for
Rafael Nadal discovered on Court No.1
that Muller was a highly-talented
player who was heading strongly
towards the world's top 50. "These
results used to happen to me two
years [ago] on clay," Nadal said.
"I think that when you're developing,
you're evolving also. I have to learn to
live the moment." Not only did Nadal
promise he would be a better grass
court player the following year –
"I'm having a court built at home in
Majorca" – but would also speak the
language better – "I study every night
two hours."

Gilles Muller of
Luxembourg shocks
French Open champion
Rafael Nadal

take them, it represented a good
opportunity spurned. And, against
players of Dechy's class, they do not
come around that often. Eventually, the
Lancashire lass managed only three
games and wondered what might be in
store next time around.

"You've got to remember, this girl is
what, 220 places above me. I don't play
these girls every week, and for me to
step onto court against her is a really
big deal. Next week, I'll go and play
a tournament in Felixville in the middle
of nowhere and play girls who are 500
in the world who play completely
differently. I've got to be realistic,
to take the positives out of each match
and know that two months ago, I'd
have got nowhere near Dechy off the
ground. I've improved an awful lot
in that time."

What had been looked upon as
a potential humdinger of a match
between Maria Sharapova, the champion,
and a teenage wannabee challenger,
Sesil Karatantcheva of Bulgaria, petered
out into a predictable, dull encounter
indeed. Sharapova was in trouble once,
when she was 15-40 down in her
opening service game, but she soon
bared her gritted teeth and
Karatantcheva duly folded. The 15-year-
old could only manage a single game.

Three seeds in the bottom half of
the women's draw went out, two from
France, Virginie Razzano (32) to
wild card Cara Black of Zimbabwe,
a champion in both women's doubles
and mixed in 2004, Marion Bartoli (29)
to Jill Craybas of the USA, and, most
notably, Vera Zvonereva (11) of Russia
to Kveta Peschke of the Czech Republic. ●

QUOTE
OF THE DAY

Wayne Arthurs, of Australia,
who lost 14-12 in the fifth set
to Germany's Alexander Popp
after four hours of tennis when
asked where he put the result
in his career of highs and lows:
"Pretty high as a low."

DAY FIVE
24.6.05

RODDICK
vs
BRACCIALI

GIMELSTOB
vs
HEWITT

MONFILS
vs
ANCIC

LOPEZ
vs
SAFIN

MYSKINA
vs
JANKOVIC

MAURESMO
vs
PERRY

Friday, June 24

ANDY RODDICK HAD BEGUN TO DEVELOP a twitch – followed by a hard stare – when people mentioned his recent five set record. Coming into Wimbledon, he had lost his five previous matches that had gone the distance, a record he was not particularly enamoured with for it posed doubts about his fitness and durability.

When the second round of the men's singles paired him with Daniele Bracciali of Italy, a lucky loser from qualifying, he did not appear to have much reason to be concerned. After all, his opponent's ranking was No.120, he did not possess anything of a grand slam record and he'd certainly never seen Centre Court from the inside before.

But strange things can happen (see the 2002 Championships annual and a European lucky loser with a surname beginning with 'B' playing Pete Sampras in the second round). The match had started on Thursday evening but had been curtailed when bad light descended after Bracciali won the third set on a tie-break. Not nice words were

exchanged between the players, Bracciali obviously feeling that Roddick had influenced the umpire into suspending play by picking up his bags before the annoucement.

"I said a bad word," Roddick admitted later. "I was walking off and he was throwing a fit. I'm not one to just go at people. That's not my style okay? But you try returning a 135mph serve when you can't see the ball. I don't think there's anything bad about walking off a dark tennis court because you can't see and you can't play."

When they returned on Friday, the light was not brilliant. Bracciali broke Roddick's serve in the fourth set in a game when he had made four of five first serves, and it started to drizzle. Off they came again. Now this was a serious test for the No.2 seed because Bracciali was playing fearless tennis, striking out from his bootstraps, not worried too much if the balls landed in or out. They were the worst kind of opponent.

And it was to Roddick's credit that he stayed the course, occasionally diving around like Boris Becker in his pomp, to win 7-5, 6-3, 6-7, 4-6, 6-3. "I just wanted to give him a few different looks in the fifth and make him think about his returns a little bit," Roddick said. He had survived. It's what it was all about.

Americans plunging around Centre Court was in danger of becoming a trend. Justin Gimelstob was more TV interviewer than playing professional these days but he, too, had earned a place in the main draw as a lucky loser and, in the second round, had put out Nicolas Massu, of Chile, the 29th seed and 2004 Olympic gold medallist.

His challenge, thus, was to try to de-rail the ambitions of Lleyton Hewitt. These were the banana-skin matches the leading players hoped to avoid, everything about it smelt uneasy; a dashing challenger with nothing to lose, who played an unorthodox game, ▶

Daniele Bracciali connects with a backhand

Right: The ever-combative Andy Roddick

LACOST

was unfazed by the location and went
hell for leather most of the time.

"I was trying to enjoy myself but I had
every intention of figuring out a way to
win the match," Gimelstob, the 28-year-old
from New Jersey said. When he stood at
5-5 in the first set tie-break, the American
went for one dive too many, attempting
to reach Hewitt's cracking return of a body
serve because he felt it was the only way
he could win the point. He didn't.

"It would have been nice to have put
him on the ropes a little bit," Gimelstob
added. "With him winning the first set
and knowing how badly off I was
physically, it took a lot of pressure off
him knowing I probably couldn't win

three sets from there." Hewitt ran out
a 7-6, 6-4, 7-5 winner but Gimelstob had
made him work exceptionally hard for
every point.

Simon Barnes, writing in The Times
applauded the American: "Sad to say
farewell to Gimelstob, who applauds
his opponent's shots, apologises to line
judges he has half killed with a serve,
does irony in his press conferences
and genuinely lives in the real world.
Wimbledon moves into the second week
on Monday – the real world must be
left far, far behind."

The Wimbledon junior champion,
Gael Monfils, was beginning to make an
impression in the senior ranks. Monfils

Justin Gimelstob gives his all against Lleyton Hewitt

Andy Murray is well equipped for the weather, as are the court attendants (below)

Young hopeful Gael Monfils

had won three of four boys' titles in 2004 – Andy Murray pipped him at the US Open – and was inside the top 100 already, and one had wondered how he might transfer his promise onto the main stages of the world.

A four set victory over Dominik Hrbaty, the 22nd seed from Slovakia, in the second round was encouragement for the 19-year-old from France to be champing at the bit for a tussle with Mario Ancic, the 2004 semi-finalist. His 6-3, 6-3, 6-1 defeat was accepted as part of a teenage education. "I don't talk about winning or losing, it's just a time to learn and see what I have to do to be the best maybe next year or two years

after," Monfils said. "Maybe I will like grass a little bit more in the future."

Marat Safin, having promised so much, lost in straight sets to Feliciano Lopez on Court No.1, though he regarded the whole experience as something to cherish rather than one to be cast aside. One of these days, one sincerely hoped, Safin would make good on grass. Lopez did all the right things, he played perfectly, he won 6-4, 7-6, 6-3 only to spoil it all right at the end. A debutant on the court, he started to march off after his win in the opposite direction to Safin. "I took the wrong way," he said. "Once I realised there's no door over there, I went to the other side." He'll learn.

Anastasia Myskina, the 2004
French Open champion, edged to
victory over Jelena Jankovic

No.3 seed Amelie Mauresmo cruised into the next round

It had been a pretty rotten period for Anastasia Myskina from Russia, the 2004 French Open champion. Form had all but deserted her, not least when she lost in the first round of Roland Garros, after which she admitted that her mother's serious illness at home in Moscow had meant she was struggling to concentrate fully on any sporting tasks.

Fortunately, in between the events, her mother had shown signs of recuperation, Myskina chose to play Eastbourne and came to Wimbledon with spirits more buoyant. Having come through a fierce match in the opening round against qualifer Katerina Bohmova of the Czech Republic, and a straight setter in the second, she faced the Serbian, Jelena Jankovic, the 17th seed, at the next stage.

When Myskina, seeded No.9, won the first set without dropping a game, all looked to be plain sailing, but match points drifted by in the second, when she led 5-3 and could not quite close it out: "When one, two, three go by you start thinking too much," Myskina said. "Then she served an ace on the second serve and I thought 'why did she do that?'"

Not only that, Jankovic stayed with Myskina all the way in the final set, so that a 6-0, 5-7, 10-8 success was every bit as demanding as it seemed. On her return to the locker room, though, a call was waiting. From her mother. "She told

Maria Sharapova gets some protection from the sun's rays

me she almost died, so that was not good news, but she meant because the match was so close. It is really hard on her when I play like this. But now she is really proud. And so happy."

Amelie Mauresmo of France was pretty content as well. The third seed rushed towards a 6-0, 6-2 victory over American Shenay Perry. "When my serve is there it is really effective on grass," she commented afterwards, with some

satisfaction. "And the slice backhand, not a lot of girls use this weapon."

Perry, ranked No.159, managed only one point on her own serve in the first set. It was recorded that, in the first game of the second, she did narrowly miss the tramlines with a swinging return of serve. It was swiflty pointed out that these were the tramlines on Court No.11 and not 13, where the match was being staged. But we all have days like that. ●

MATCH
OF THE DAY

Feliciano Lopez saw off Marat Safin (far left and below) in three sets

FELICIANO LOPEZ V MARAT SAFIN

It wasn't such a shock after all. Marat Safin had never felt at his best on grass and Feliciano Lopez, the tall Spaniard, moves so effortlessly across the surface, so perhaps a 6-4, 7-6, 6-3 victory for the left-hander was more an awakening of his championship prospects than a huge wave of incredulity through the local environs. The shock had more to do with the fact that Safin took defeat so well, said that it had made him think again about his adversity to grass and that he had absolutely nothing to complain about. Having pinched yourself to make sure this was the real Marat and not some moustachioed imposter, you wondered what a supremely focused Russian might achieve in 2006.

DAY SIX
25.6.05

FEDERER
vs
KIEFER

MURRAY
vs
NALBANDIAN

CLIJSTERS
vs
VINCI

TURSUNOV
vs
POPP

S. WILLIAMS
vs
CRAYBAS

SATURDAY, JUNE 25

THE WEATHER WAS DREICH – A SCOTS word that means indescribably gloomy. The temperature seemed to have plunged 20 degrees. And this first Saturday of The Championships was to promise the wind of change that those with an eye to all things British had longed for.

Andy Murray's promise had been underscored by his performances at Queen's Club – where he was within two points of defeating Thomas Johansson, the former Australian Open champion, and by the opening two rounds of Wimbledon where George Bastl and Radek Stepanek, relative tour veterans, had been defeated for the loss of not a single set. From Court No.2, to Court No.1, it was only apt that Centre should be booked for the Scot.

The delay from Friday's rain meant that Roger Federer would open the programme against Nicolas Kiefer, the bearded German, a women's match would follow before Murray would be ushered past those famed words of Kipling for the first time in his life.

As ever, the Royal Box was given over to legends of sport and entertainment. The knights of the rowing fraternity, Sir Steve Redgrave and Sir Matthew Pinsent were joined by the remaining members of the quartet James Cracknell and Ed Coode; athletes David Hemery, Denise Lewis, Mary Peters and Tessa Sanderson were acknowledged as were the special guests of Tim Phillips, the Club Chairman; Billie Jean King, six times the singles champion contributing to her record 20 titles at Wimbledon across all events, and Tony Trabert, also from the United States, who had won the men's ▶

Top: Roger Federer bids farewell to Nicolas Kiefer
Right: Sean Connery leads the applause for young compatriot, Andrew Murray (over)

Above: Andy Murray gave everything in an energy-sapping, five-set epic against David Nalbandian

Right: The Argentine closes in on an emotional victory

Below: The respect was mutual

singles five decades earlier. On the front right of the box was Sir Sean Connery, the actor who defined James Bond, and a fellow Scot obviously enamoured at the prospect of watching the 18-year-old from Dunblane moved into the exalted circles of tennis.

Federer against Kiefer was a longer hors d'ouevre than had been anticipated. The champion had not quite found his stride as yet and he knew that Kiefer had a reputation for playing brilliant tennis when the mood took him; and that he was the scalp, the champion on Centre Court, that every professional wanted to have.

The Swiss started ferociously, taking the first set in double quick time but Kiefer could be a cussed opponent, who had reached four grand slam quarter-finals, and realised on this cold and dank afternoon, that if he kept plugging away, Federer might not find it quite so easy to plug into the free-flowing tennis that is his norm.

He said he should have won straight sets but Kiefer sneaked the second set tie break and having taken the third set, the Swiss was a break down in the fourth. "If I win in five, spend five hours on court, or in one hour, it doesn't matter, as long as I keep winning," the champion said on his 6-2, 6-7, 6-1, 7-5 victory. "I had to survive some tough moments but those are good for me. I am through the first week."

The mood and emphasis changed for the second match – the court emptied somewhat and Kim Clijsters, the No.15 seed and Eastbourne champion, stepped out to meet the unseeded Roberta Vinci, the world No.111 from Italy. Clijsters may have dropped serve for the first time – and in the first game – but it did not stop her moving just as smoothly on Centre as she had in the grass court warm up on the South Coast. Near the end of the match there was a palpable sense of excitement in the crowd. They wanted to see the young hero about whom they were reading more and more.

He walked on as if stumbling into his bedroom – and he has the reputation for laying things down in his house and never bothering to pick them up again. The iPod was stuck into his left ear, he had his towels in an unpretentious plastic bag (the supermarket check out kind) and it did not look as if an iron had been anywhere near his kit.

Initially, he was nervous, as one might expect. Nalbandian won his first service game without drawing sweat (and he is a man who sweats copiously). But there was trouble ahead as he tried a under-slice drop shot that presented break points, the second of which the Briton accepted with a raking forehand winner. Nalbandian responded well but in a flurry of five service breaks in ten games, the first set entered a tie-break.

These are the situations in which experience would normally thrive but, the first point apart, Nalbandian trailed, Murray played sudden death with a veteran's poise, great net reactions, aces, drop shots by jove and finally, he extracted a forehand service return from the Argentine into the net. A set to the ▶

DMITRY TURSUNOV v ALEXANDER POPP

Having disposed of Tim Henman in the second round, it would have been easy for Dmitry Tursunov to have swiftly disappeared at the next stage but, instead, having dropped the first set to the giant former quarter-finalist from Germany, his response was dramatic. For the first time in his grand slam career, he was into the second week, one of only two non seeds in the men's draw to reach the fourth round. And this because, after he had won the second set tie-break 7-5, he, metaphorically "went to the bathroom, looked in the mirror and slapped myself a couple of times. It seemed to work." Tursunov won 5-7, 7-6, 6-2, 6-2 and must have been the only player still in the event with just two free rackets in his bag.

good, he took a toilet break, leaving Nalbandian to contemplate an interesting afternoon.

The second set provided a vivid glimpse of Murray's potential, he won it emphatically 6-1. And Murray had points in each of the first three games to have led 3-0 in the third, which would surely have been curtains. But Nalbandian was rallying, using discernably more power off the ground and bounding across the turf with greater purpose. The screw was being turned in that a prospective 3-0 lead for murray became a real 3-0 advantage for Nalbandian, which swiftly became 6-0, in a manner that suggested Murray was tiring.

The fourth was to become special indeed. Whatever he had conserved at the tail end of the third set, enabled Murray to leap back into the fray in the fourth, in which he broke first to lead 2-1, survived two break points from two netted forehands and did not once seem fazed by the growing clamour around him, indeed he was urging the crowd to lift him to more improbable shot-making.

But Nalbandian is regarded as one of the most intelligent match players in world tennis and he struck at what looked like an opportune moment, as Murray served for a 5-3 lead. He led 40-15 in the next game but Murray would not be ▶

Long goodbyes: While Andy Murray milks the adulation on Centre Court (above), Serena Williams (below) can't hide her humiliation at losing to Jill Craybas

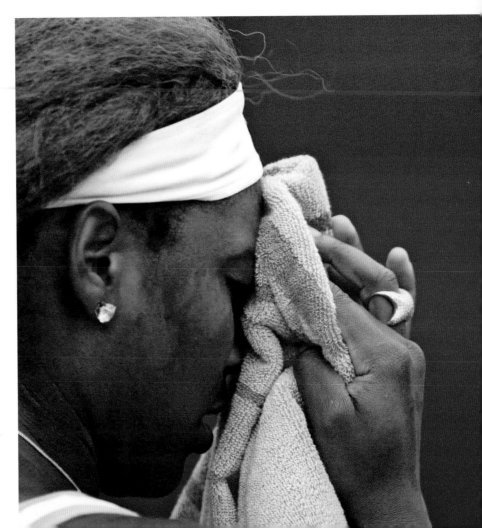

A tennis ball waits
to be propelled at
140mph by Andy
Roddick's serve

QUOTE
OF THE DAY

**Andy Murray after his defeat
to David Nalbandian:**
*"I think walking off Centre
Court, knowing I had just lost
a match, and the noise that
everybody made and the support
they gave me, it made me feel
I almost belonged there. And
hopefully, it's going to continue,
me playing on Centre Court,
more often in the future."*

**To Guillermo Coria
of Argentina:**
Q: *You, fourth round.*
A: *Unbelievable.*

moved and forced his way to three break points. The second may always haunt him for a second serve down the T landed plumb in his hitting zone be his forehand return was netted. Imagine had he been able to serve for the match.

Nalbandian survived, broke to love for the set and lost only a further game, though Murray did not let up on a single point. "My legs are really, really knackered, I couldn't move towards the end," he said. "I was annoyed I couldn't keep running in the fifth set because I was moving round well in the fourth. I just know I can play well and compete with some of the best guys. I'm not as strong as them which is understandable when you think I'm just 18. The more five set matches I play, physically I'm bound to be better."

The Centre Court programme had been scheduled to run to four matches but, as the clock ticked towards 7.30pm, the decision was taken to shift the match between Serena Williams and Jill Craybas to Court No.2. The Committee probably surmised that it would not take their former champion too long to brush aside a player who was ranked No.85 in the world and who had not been beyond the first round in 17 of her previous 24 grand slam appearances.

Well, they were right on one point, the match did not take that long. But astonishingly it was Craybas who emerged with the spoils, winning 6-3, 7-6, striking the ball as well as she could have ever done in her life, sticking to the plan of trying not to give Serena too much pace and having one of those days when the ball seems to strike the middle of the racket on every other shot.

"Can you tell us what you thought about your game today?" Serena was asked. "I can't use those words," she replied. "I think I was better off staying at home for sure. She just got balls back, she didn't do anything exceptionally well. I couldn't win a service game in the first set, then it was downhill."

The rest of what had been a remarkable day was rather predictable, with wins for Venus Williams (who would meet Craybas next), Mary Pierce, Lindsay Davenport, Nathalie Dechy and Maria Sharapova. Amen to predictability. ●

See you Monday: Maria Sharapova and (below) Mary Pierce ease into the second week

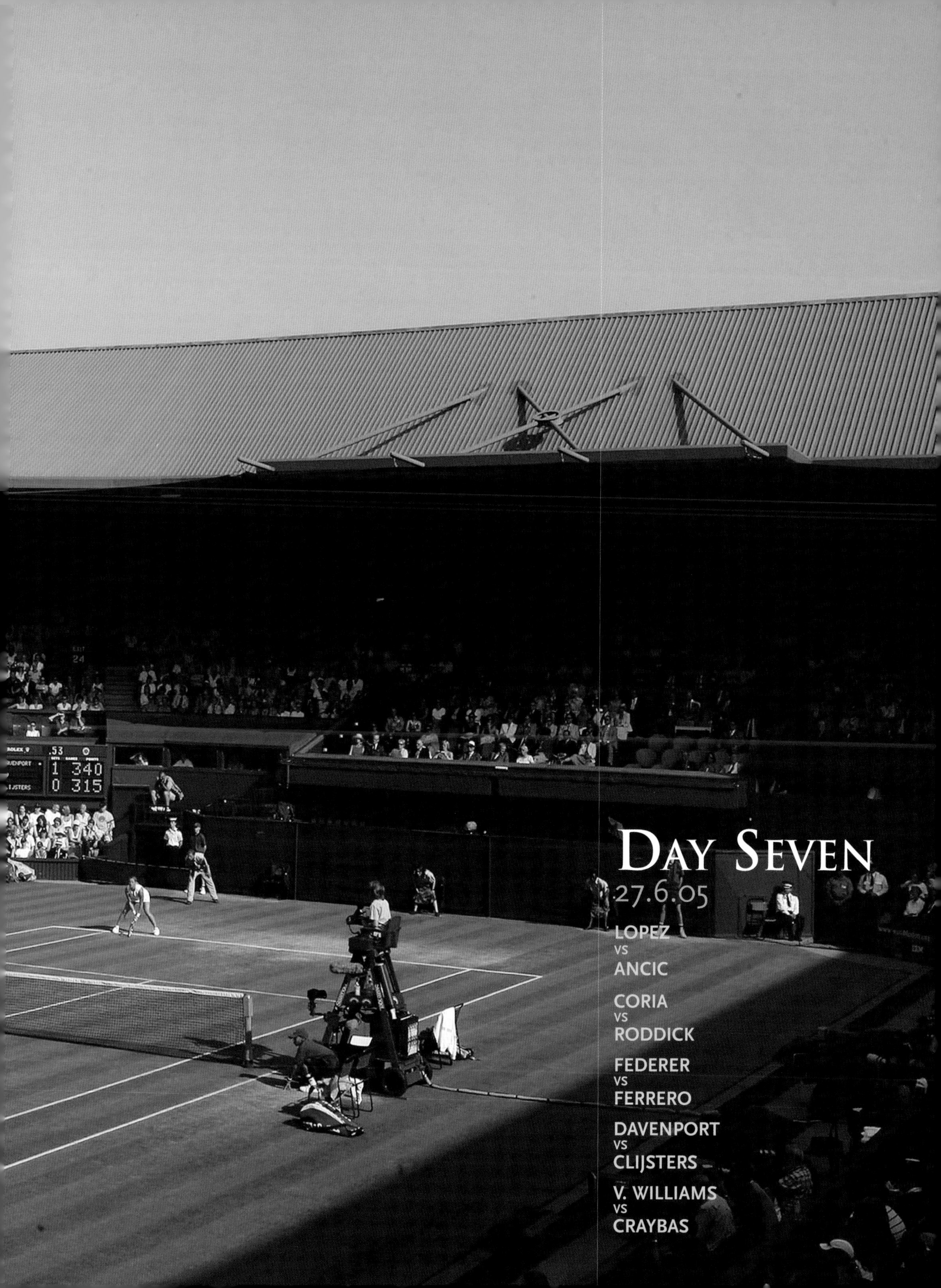

DAY SEVEN

27.6.05

LOPEZ
VS
ANCIC

CORIA
VS
RODDICK

FEDERER
VS
FERRERO

DAVENPORT
VS
CLIJSTERS

V. WILLIAMS
VS
CRAYBAS

Monday,
June 27

IT IS ARGUABLY THE FINEST DAY IN THE entire tennis calendar, the second Monday of The Championships; eight men's and eight women's fourth round matches, reams of pure talent, superstars with racket bags draped across their shoulders whizzing through the concourse, security guards, twisting heads everywhere, all taking stock, nudging friends, wondering if that really was the Feliciano, Fernando, Juan Carlos, Anastasia or Amelie they had seen in the papers. You daren't look away for a moment.

There was not a breathing space to be found around Court No.18 where Spain's Feliciano Lopez opened against Mario Ancic of Croatia, a testosterone tussle if ever there was one. Lopez, brought up on the hard courts of Madrid, had been to the fourth round of Wimbledon twice before. Ancic had defeated Tim Henman on his way to the semi-finals in 2004, so there was plenty of grass court pedigree on display.

All the talk of a Hispanic hue before the tournament had centred on the potential of Rafael Nadal to transfer his ▶

Mario Ancic lunges into a volley.
Left: Roger Federer prepares to
slam down another ace

clay court animation to grass. Lopez's
qualities had been inappropriately
overlooked, for here was a natural
grass court player, six foot two inches,
and a big game to match. Ancic knew
he had his work cut out.

One of Lopez's favourite sayings is
"this is not Bambi" as in, suspend the
dream world, take a reality check. Well,
after a 6-4, 6-2, 6-2 victory a Spanish
serve and volleyer found himself in the
quarter-finals of the men's singles for
the first time since 1966. Bambi lived.

Manuel Orantes had been the last,
in 1972, but he was more a durable clay
court player who outlasted Ion Tiriac in
five sets in the fourth round, lost four
games to Australian Colin Dibley in the
quarters before falling to Ilie Nastase
in the semis. Lopez was a real change,
with a graceful ease of movement and
an intuitive understanding of when to
venture forward and when to exchange
from the back.

When Lopez was a kid, he suffered
numerous allergies and doctors told his
mother, Belen, a nurse, that he should
take up swimming. Such was his talent

for the sport – especially at the freestyle
and butterfly – he was almost tempted
by an athletic scholarship at an
American university. But he was
a terrific tennis player as well, and
tennis won out. What was remarkable
was that since reaching the semi-finals
at the ATP stop in Marseille in February,
he had only won back-to-back matches
once, on clay in Estoril. Perhaps his
situation was helped in that David
Sherwood, the British wild card, rather
froze in the second round but Lopez
went on to defeat Marat Safin in the
third round and cantered beyond Ancic.

"This is the way I play, and have for
many years now," he said. "I'm probably
not the typical Spanish player, but I still
like to play from the baseline as well.
But, for sure, one of my best weapons
is to serve and volley, no? The first time
I had ever played on grass was my first
Wimbledon, actually [2002], and
I reached the fourth round. I realise
straight away I can play well on grass."

As did David Nalbandian, when
he stepped out for his first grass
championship, the 2002 Wimbledon,

The Feliciano Lopez show
goes on with a win over
Mario Ancic, while
Guillermo Coria (right) is
felled by Andy Roddick

and surged all the way to the final. He was described by Rick Broadbent in *The Times* after his convincing straight set victory over Richard Gasquet, the supremely talented French teenager, as "dry rot, grinding down his opponents with an insidious attack."

Nalbandian could not be further removed from Lopez in terms of technique and approach if he tried. For the Argentine, the baseline hug is the crux, and though there have been mutterings in the past about what appears like a bit of a belly on him, his speed across the court demolishes the theory he's not 100 per cent fit.

Lopez loped. But he was able to smother the Croat's ambition 6-4, 6-4, 6-2 – a model of organisation and calm tenacity, although it must have been a source of inspiration that he found his opponent in a bit of a strop and soon afterwards, a trough. Ancic handed Lopez no fewer than 15 double faults, which would have been sloppy even if the Spaniard was not having one of those days when volleys fizzed off his racket and passes dinged against the lines.

Of the 16 men left, five spoke with Spanish as their native tongue. Lopez, Nalbandian and Fernando Gonzalez of Chile were to take a further stride, but it was to be the end of the grass court rainbow for Juan Carlos Ferrero and Guillermo Coria. Both had, in their time, bucked the trend of Latin indifference to Wimbledon, listening at first to siren voices of discontent about grass but determined – as professionals should be – to find out for themselves

if it was all bad. Ferrero, a former French Open champion, had had a difficult year, striving to overcome the effects of chicken pox. When it first hit him, "I felt like I was really going to die, I had never been so bad in my life." The road back was hard. When an athlete in his prime is stripped of full health, it eats away at his confidence and Ferrero was struggling to become the player he once was.

What happens when you aren't feeling exactly tickety-boo? Along comes a fourth round draw at Wimbledon against Roger Federer. There was a headline in one newspaper on Monday morning that said "I can stop the champ". Well, he gave himself a decent chance. Ferrero played well, at times extremely well, but not well enough – a feeling most players had against Federer. "When the matches ▶

Venus avenges her sister by beating Serena's conqueror Jill Craybas (above)

LINDSAY DAVENPORT
V KIM CLIJSTERS

Lindsay Davenport said she felt that certain players
were running her out of the sport in 2002, 2003 and
a bit of 2004. She had lost many times in a row to
Venus Williams and her record against Kim Clijsters
was not all that good. But, in a fourth round at
Wimbledon, when faced with a player who has been
to grand slam finals, it was important that the world
No.1 raised her game. "It's very rare I pat myself on
the back," she said, but when confronted with the
fact that 37 per cent of her serves were unreturned
"especially on grass you need free points," she said
– the American had every reason to be pleased.
"I just stuck where I wanted to go and knew what
I wanted to do," she added on her 6-3, 6-7, 6-3
victory. There were plenty who were delighted to
see Clijsters out of the way.

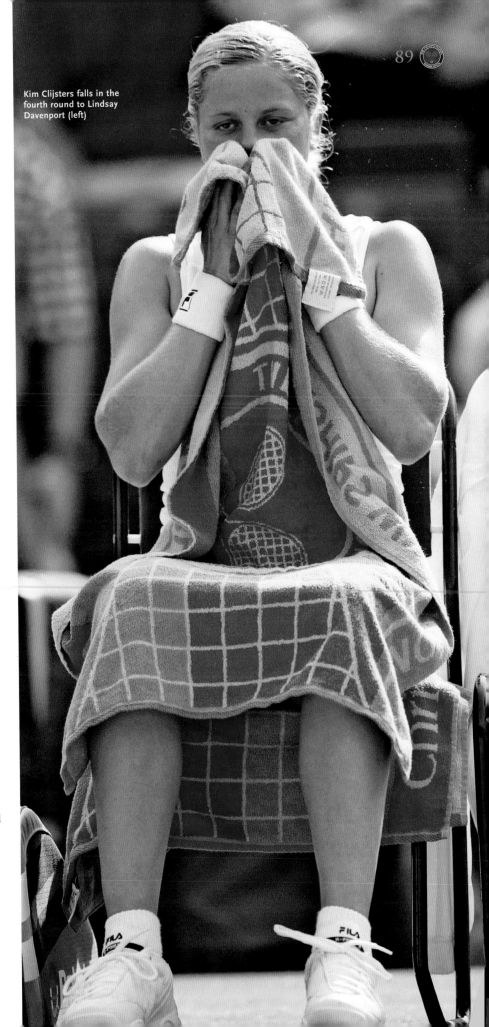

Kim Clijsters falls in the fourth round to Lindsay Davenport (left)

are so close," Ferrero said after his 6-3, 6-4, 7-6 defeat, "he plays at the same level all the time, no mistakes, no important mistakes on important points. He holds his concentration all the time."

Coria, still seeking the grand slam title that would cement his place in the sport's hierarchy, lost in straight sets to Andy Roddick, 6-3, 7-6, 6-4, a match that, like Ferrero against Federer, hinged on one or two better shots at critical times.

Over on Court No.2, where the matches tend to have added electricity because of the closeness of the public, Venus Williams was happily indulging in a little bit of family retribution. Jill Craybas probably expected as much; it is not good for one's health to defeat one Williams sister and return to the same piece of land a couple of days later and have to take on the other one.

"I had a good position to be the second sister," Venus said of her 6-0, 6-2 crunching of Craybas. "I was doing a little bit for her but mostly I was doing this for me." Off she went to be asked more questions about scarves and headdresses and Serena and the London bid for the Olympics. Such is Venus's lot.

The match that might well decide the ladies championship duly arrived and duly lived up to everyone's expectations. Lindsay Davenport had stunned herself – and certainly Kim Clijsters – by turning around a 6-1, 3-1 deficit in the French Open a month earlier. The rematch was every bit as unrelenting, no preen, no nonsense, just a mutual attempt to smash tennis balls to a pulp.

It was described as tennis with nothing added and nothing taken away. Clijsters saved a match point in the second set tie-break, which she won by the simple means of playing the bigger points a touch better. The pattern continued with Davenport dominant and Clijsters defiant until, inexplicably, the bottom fell out of the world for the Belgian when she served three double faults in a single game to toss away the match. A lot of people I saw after the match said this should have been the final, which is a great compliment," Clijsters said. "I need to get my seeding up so I don't have to face these kind of matches in the fourth round." ●

DAY EIGHT
28.6.05

SHARAPOVA
vs
PETROVA

V. WILLIAMS
vs
PIERCE

MYSKINA
vs
MAURESMO

DAVENPORT
vs
KUZNETSOVA

Amelie Mauresmo
bludgeons her way into
the second week

TUESDAY, JUNE 28

THOSE TRAVELLING IN THE ENVIRONS OF London SW19 on the second Tuesday may have had cause to slam on the brakes, wind down their car windows and check they had heard what they thought they had heard. Was it a bird, was it a plane, or was it Super Shriek?

Giles Smith in *The Times* likened it, at its most extreme, to "the noise an owl might make were you to hit it hard with a stick." Maria Sharapova was the culprit, revving up the noise levels on Court No.1 to reach the semi-finals for a second successive year, defeating Nadia Petrova, her Russian compatriot, in straight sets. Across St Mary's Walk, on Centre, there was plenty of shrieking effort as Venus Williams filled the air with growls as Mary Pierce was put to the sword.

It was never this way when Françoise Durr was feathering the ball, the pavements did not shudder to the anguished cries of Christine Truman or Betsy Nagelsen. No, Monica Seles was the instigator of the tennis shriek and my, haven't these girls taken the story on a few chapters?

Sharapova against Petrova would likely be a bit feisty, given that the defending champion and few of her fellow Russians had not seen totally eye to eye. In Carson, California, a couple of years ago, according to eye-witnesses, Yuri – Sharapova's father – claimed that Petrova had responded to his daughter's fist pumping at the start of the third set with "an unladylike gesture". Yuri then taunted Petrova for the rest of the match and upset her coach so much he pushed Yuri into a rubbish bin before security guards intervened. Needle was expected.

Sharapova had won 21 matches in succession on grass, and conceded only 17 games en route to the last eight. Petrova was a semi-finalist at Roland Garros before losing to Justine Henin-Hardenne. She may have reached No.8 in the world on the Sony Ericsson WTA Tour, but she had not yet won a title. ▶

And the shriek goes on:
Sharapova let's everyone know
she's at the top of her game

She may not have quite been at her imperious best in The Championships to date but knew that this would be a genuine test. Forget Petrova's unhappy knack of stumbling when adjacent to a winning post, there was a match to be won and, in the first set, Sharapova found herself under greater pressure than she had been at any time in her defence thus far.

The battle between these big-serving heavy hitters produced a first set so tight it seemed for a while that it would need explosives to loosen it. Even though the players had to cope with a swirling breeze, performing its own version of a Mexican wave around the court's bowl-shaped arena and threatening to introduce an unwelcome random element, we had to wait until the ninth game before anyone opened up even a two point lead against service, let alone get to break point.

Petrova was launching serves up to 114mph, Sharapova was doing the boxer's shuffle she does before settling down into her service action, and was coming back just as strongly and even more accurately. Petrova had discovered that Sharapova's second serve was highly attackable but if she didn't attack it hard, she was soon back on the defensive.

It took 55 minutes for the first set to be nudged to its conclusion – Sharapova won a thrilling tie-break 8-6 – the rest of the match would disappear in a half-hour gulp. A glorious running volley gave Sharapova the break and the match seemed to be passing into the formality of held serves until, in the process of serving to close it out, Sharapova mysteriously handed Petrova a chance to break back with her only double fault of the set. But the champion's next shot caught the net cord so firmly, the ball actually appeared to stop on her side of the net before dropping on the other side. But that, perhaps, was the mark of the champion, luck when you don't especially need it.

"I told the ball to hit the net and roll over, that's what comes with experience," she said later. "It's been important for me to learn from different situations in the past year, whether it is winning or losing," she said. "Even in tough situations, when I am down as far as the score is concerned, I don't feel down mentally. I'm very tough." And loud.

Across the way, Venus Williams spent 25 minutes not losing a game to Mary Pierce in the opening set of her quarter-final, and it seemed as if Mary, as she had done in a distinctly uneasy French Open final, would offer the resistance of a blancmange.

One of Pierce's many affectations is to strike what artists like to call a "vigorous pose" in moments of disappointment and to hold it long enough for a couple of preliminary sketches. She also, as one correspondent put it, "walked from place to place in a trance of beauty, as if she expected orchids to spring up at her feet at every step".

In the second set, those orchids would have been crushed beneath her feet for the former French and Australian champion roused herself and began to hit deep and hit hard. Williams, having already won the match in her mind, suddenly lost the certainty in her groundstrokes and the killer grip she'd had on the match began to be released.

Williams then began to roar the place down, as Pierce matched her stroke for stroke, winner for winner, point for point, game for game. You kept waiting for Williams to put the game away decisively, but, all of a sudden, she was not in such a decisive frame of mind. Besides, Pierce was now playing some seriously good stuff herself, although, not surprisingly, errors were dotted about like boiled sweet wrappers in the front row of the Royal Box.

Pierce actually had a couple of set points and, on the second of them, opened the court up perfectly, only to play the worst drive volley you will see. ▶

Anastasia Myskina loses out to Mauresmo

Eventually, once Williams got herself organised, Pierce couldn't cope but the second set lasted an hour longer than the first, Williams winning 6-0, 7-6 (12-10). "I was hitting a lot of good shots or hard shots in the tie-break, I wasn't moon-balling it over and she was hitting winners out of nowhere. After facing five set points or what have you [yes, it was but Venus had been noted before for losing the score in tie-breaks, remember last year's second round?], that was just a great win.

"I think being in the semi-finals is my normal ranking, it's where I belong. I lost a lot of points in the clay court season, I couldn't go to some tournaments to defend points so I fell out of the top ten because of that, too. Then I didn't play great at the French."

Pierce, good on her, wanted to come back and try again. "This is my seventeenth year and I want to play a few more but I can't honestly see many of the girls wanting to play ten, 15, 20 years now, because the game is so much more demanding. The matches are a lot more difficult, a lot more physically demanding and there are a lot more of them."

The Russian contingent had been reduced to one, for Anastasia Myskina was beaten in straight sets, 6-3, 6-4, by Amelie Mauresmo of France and the quarter-final line was completed when Lindsay Davenport defeated Svetlana Kuznetsova, also in two sets.

There was a stirred up full house on Court No.2 – when was there not? – when four rather elderly gentlemen made their way through the clamouring throng. Enter John McEnroe, Peter Fleming (the second not looking a day older than when he could call McEnroe "junior" and get away with it), John Lloyd and John Feaver. It was not members' privileges, but the over-45s doubles. McEnroe was wearing a floral bandanna and a copy of Rafael Nadal's "pirata" trousers, so obviously his wife wasn't in town to tell him how daft they looked on him.

Lloyd, bless him, could hardly move, Feaver served a couple of his torpedoes, but Fleming and McEnroe triumphed 6-3, 6-4. The crowd whooped it up. ●

Team America: Venus Williams (above) and Lindsay Davenport (left) reach the semi-finals

QUOTE
OF THE DAY

Venus Williams:

"I'm like a zombie. I can't wake up in the mornings. But I hate to go to bed at night. And I need at least eight hours sleep. Sometimes I just don't get up. I just watch The Golden Girls."

Maria Sharapova:

Q: *You like going down in Wimbledon history?*
A: *"Oh yeah, for sure. To be in that musuem, obviously it's a big achievement."*

FEDERER
VS
GONZALEZ

HEWITT
VS
LOPEZ

JOHANSSON
VS
NALBANDIAN

RODDICK
VS
GROSJEAN

WEDNESDAY, JUNE 29

NEARING THE END OF A FASCINATING DAY of men's quarter-finals, the pealing of the bell that announces the arrival of a player in the interview room tolled. But each of the eight players in the singles had been filtered through, so who was heading in for an evening chat? Enter Todd Woodbridge.

The record-breaking nine-time Wimbledon doubles champion had chosen to retire. How could this be? He looked as impressionable and fresh-faced as he had been when he made his Wimbledon debut in the first round in 1989, when he happened to become the first player to defeat Pete Sampras on the hallowed lawns. Could Woodbridge,

who won six times with his compatriot Mark Woodforde and three with Jonas Bjorkman, the Swede, really have had enough of the grind of the tour, at 34?

He and Mahesh Bhupathi of India, seeded six, had lost in straight sets in the second round to Steven Huss of Australia and Wesley Moodie of South Africa, a pair of qualifiers. "My partnership did not go as well as I would have hoped," Woodbridge said. "I didn't come to this tournament planning to retire but I have had so many good, strong memories here, it was the right place to do it and the right time in my career to do it.

"In doubles, you've got to choose good partners and you've got to be there at the right time. People are always going to argue whether I was the best or not but I think I have a pretty good case that I was the best forehand court player of all time. I can at least take that home with me. And this place holds the best memories I've had, from the first time I played a junior match, a singles semi, a mixed title, all of my greatest results came here. I came here and felt I was absolutely at ease. Mentally, I focused better and kept my temper in check. Everything I did was very purposeful."

Like almost every Australian who had walked through the gates of the club, Wimbledon was an inspiring place for Woodbridge. He would be missed, not only as a player, but as one of those really good blokes for whom nothing was ever too much. See you mate.

One image was plastered all across the back pages on Thursday morning because it was impossible for picture ▶

The imposing figure of Roger Federer closing in on the ball

Left: Veteran Todd Woodbridge before announcing his retirement

editors to resist the story it told. It had Roger Federer, racket thrust forward, about two feet off the ground, at the exact moment of his 7-5, 6-2, 7-6 victory over Fernando Gonzalez of Chile. It was the champion personified.

Gonzalez played out of his skin but Federer was out of this world. He took the big hitting style of the man from Santiago and turned it into a weapon against the man who wielded it. He did so without malice, without animosity, almost with an air of reluctance. As he did so, he created patterns and cross patterns. Invariably, he could not take the initiative against someone so determined to hit a winner every time the ball came over the net. But any style Federer chose, he used to delight himself and the crowd.

Boris Becker, the three time champion wrote: "There is no game plan to beat Roger Federer, such a thing doesn't exist. Federer has not lost on a grass court for three years, when he loses a set there is an investigation, as if something has to be terribly wrong. Fernando Gonzalez played as well as he could in the quarter-final, he probably exceeded any expectation of how he would play and he lost in straight sets. Why? Because Federer came up with shots the like of which I have not seen before (and I've seen a few), shots you cannot practice. He made drop shots from impossible positions, winners from nowhere, he made more "gets" that I have seen in my life.

"When the two players walked up to shake hands at the end, the look on Gonzalez's face spoke of sheer admiration for the player he had lost to. I can share in that. I spent time with Federer this morning and to say he is

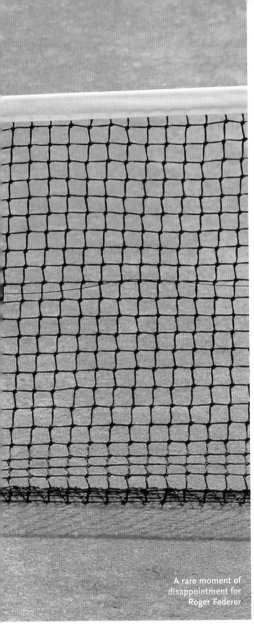

A rare moment of disappointment for Roger Federer

Fernado Gonzalez lunges despairingly for the ball

the essence of calm and relaxation understates the mood of serenity in which he lives his life. He had enough time for everyone, a word for everyone, he not only has the potential to be the greatest player the sport has seen but he is its finest salesman as well. What more could tennis want – how much more will tennis get?" It was a fascinating poser.

The other three men's quarter-finals may not have contained such sublime tennis as produced by the Swiss ace, but each game nevertheless had enough magic and mystery to titillate the most discerning tennis watcher.

Intriguingly, for the third year running, eight different nations were represented in the men's quarters and there was no unseeded player at this stage for the first time since 1975 – even given the fact that the seeds were raised from 16 to 32 in 2001.

Lleyton Hewitt battles on

Left: Feliciano Lopez
stoops for a backhand

Below left: Mutual respect
at the end of the game

Lleyton Hewitt, in company with
Federer the only former champion left,
was facing Feliciano Lopez, the only
left-hander standing, in a fabulous
contrast of styles: the dig-your-toes-in
feistiness of the Australian against
Lopez, who appeared to play in semi-
slow motion – one man who was in
a constant state of fidget, the other
who, even when he yanked his shorts
up over his thighs to receive serve, did
so in a manner that it might have been
set to music.

In the play itself, when Lopez was
good, he was very, very good. When he
was bad, he was awful. He was handed
the chance to take the first set on a plate
when Hewitt dropped serve in the fifth
game, a double fault, woeful volley and,
finally, a net cord ganging up on him.
But Lopez handed the initiative back in
the eighth, slicing a high backhand into
the tram-lines because he did not move
his feet well enough, before throwing in
a double fault of his own. Then, serving
at 6-5, he dumped two lazy forehands in
succession, flopped with another high
backhand volley and, having responded
with two huge service winners, contrived

Thomas Johansson
surprises David
Nalbandian

to net a forehand half-volley off his shoes, venturing too tepidly behind what he thought would be another unreturnable serve.

The second set continued along a rather mundane path until, when he needed to keep everything together, Lopez became too lax, dropping serve and the set in the tenth game, with more double faults, volleys that lacked real urgency and slices of insufficient slice. The third set tie-break was something of a formality.

"Lleyton is a big player, no?" Lopez said, clearly meaning size of reputation rather than his stature. "Everything he is doing, he is doing good. I think he did 12 unforced errors in the whole match. That is an interesting thing to see. It was a nice, nice day for me to play on Centre Court for the first time, the nerves didn't let me play bad. I played the way I wanted to play and that is what I will do in the next tournaments."

Not a lot had either been heard, or made of Thomas Johansson of Sweden up until this point in The

Championships. Though he had reached the semi-finals of the Stella Artois championships at Queen's Club, and was a past winner of the Nottingham Open, he was significantly underrated by those who should have known better.

His 7-6, 6-2, 6-2 triumph over David Nalbandian in the match most thought would be the longest of the quarter-finals, was illustrative of the depth of his ability. Once he took the first set on the tie-break, he did not give Nalbandian a sniff. "The way I was hitting the ball felt really good," he said. "I could go for my shots when I wanted to. This is one of the best weeks of my life." ▶

Venus Williams
and Mark Knowles
in the mixed doubles

Former semi-finalist Sebastien Grosjean posed a real threat to Andy Roddick (below and right)

ANDY RODDICK
V SEBASTIEN GROSJEAN

Sebastien Grosjean had been a semi-finalist in his two previous Wimbledons, the second of which he lost to Andy Roddick – he had also been beaten by Roddick in the quarter-final at Queen's, but he had never played a five-set match at Wimbledon before this year and had already survived two. For Roddick too, with the weight of expectation squarely on his shoulders, this was a vital match and when he lost the first set rather too quickly, it seemed as if he might fold beneath it all. He surged through the second and third sets but faltered, barely, but enough for Grosjean to find a way back into the match with his exquisite changes of pace and fierce forehands. The fifth set was quite probably the best he had played since the first in last year's final. It needed to be. The American won 3-6, 6-2, 6-1, 3-6, 6-3. ●

DAY TEN
30.6.05

SHARAPOVA
VS
V. WILLIAMS

DAVENPORT
VS
MAURESMO

THURSDAY, JUNE 30

THE ELECTRONIC CLOCK ON CENTRE Court, whose yellow figuring was easy to pick out in the gathering gloom, had just ticked past 5pm. The announcement was made, first to jeers and then cheers. Because of the light rain that had fallen since mid-morning, no play had been possible. It was one of those incredibly taxing afternoons – for those with tickets, especially, but also in the press room wondering how on earth we were going to fill the pages of the morning papers without a tennis ball having been struck.

The tones of club chief executive Chris Gorringe, having previously delivered

Right: Venus Williams avoids the showers to reach another Wimbledon final

dreary prognostications from the London Weather Centre (one wonders what the telephone charges amount to between the two places during the two weeks), had a perkiness that had been missing previously. "There is going to be a change of schedule," he announced. "One semi-final will be moved to Court No.1, the other will be played on Centre Court." Cue levels of jeering which, down in his announcer's cubbyhole, Gorringe would quite possibly not have heard. "The match on Centre Court will be Miss Sharapova..." he did not have to announce the opponent's name for the cat-calling to cease and wild celebrations to begin "... against Miss Williams."

And so the crowd settled down and waited. And waited. Umpire Alison Lang walked on to mighty applause, climbed into her chair and told the assembly they would have to wait a further ten minutes "given the change of schedule".

Ten minutes became close to 20. Alan Mills, the referee, having come to the side of the court to unclip the netting that allows unfettered access to the court, spun on his heel and walked back a couple of paces, tossed his head back slightly and gave one of those "where are they?" looks.

Finally, Miss Sharapova in long pants, Miss Williams in regulation attire, came striding on as if they were the ones who had been kept waiting. As they warmed up, the clouds got so dark it seemed as if it must rain again, but mercifully, they blew away and combat was joined. I used the word combat advisedly.

Each player set about trying to seize control, neither keen on backing down. It was clear from the outset that every aspect of this fascinating encounter was going to be fiercely disputed. Much had been made during the event of such matters as grunting and press conference put-downs, and both players had done admirably in each of these departments. But the only way to really claim the high ground in women's tennis is by weight and depth of ground stroke, backed up by weight and depth of personality. ▶

These were opponents altogether worthy of each other's steel. Both are champions, both saw themselves as champions and both believed they had a right to some kind of hegemony over Centre Court.

Williams had been speaking openly about the lessening of her commitment to tennis, which, if she did not say it, was not her utmost priority any more, even if she still spoke of it warmly. Her tennis, and her interest in it, had been patchy. A third-round defeat to Bulgarian 16-year-old Sesil Karatantcheva in the French Open preceded a raft of debate about whether she was a spent force in grand slam terms.

Quite how she had managed to play herself into such astonishing form, only she and those really close to her would appreciate; but the fact that she, a proper champion, was facing a younger champion would certainly have stirred her blood. The efforts of both girls was unrelenting, their control of shots remarkable because of the blurring pace of the ball from the turf. Williams was a woman inspired and it was Sharapova who had done the inspiring.

Suddenly we were witnessing the rebirth of Venus, every roaring, belting martial inch of her and she had a mission to demonstrate to the court, and to a certain Russian princess with an underarm deodorant contract, that these things count for little in the biggest scheme of things.

The titanic first set went to a tie-break and here Williams, who had been consistently more aggressive in her shot selection and more adventurous in her approach, moved ahead. She played as if she had nothing to lose, which, of course, she had. "For me it was just one point at a time, just sticking to my game and not losing focus," she said. If Sharapova upped the pace a notch, Venus found another. The tie-break pocketed she broke the Russian to love in the first game of the second set and never really looked back. ▶

Suits you: Sharapova dons long trousers for Wimbledon's inclement weather

Miss L. DAVENPORT

v

Miss A. MAURESMO

Williams won 7-6, 6-1, though she would admit that the decisive nature of the second set score did not truly reflect the typically Sharapova-like endeavour the Russian put into each point. "Credit to her for making me play at the best level I could find today," Sharapova said. "She was serving consistently big, and I didn't think I was serving that big. I'm always ready for a tough match, this is normal. Why would anyone be here if they didn't want to be the best."

Over on Court No.1, Lindsay Davenport and Amelie Mauresmo, having initially been the first match on Centre were through their first three games before the lid was lifted on Sharapova and Williams. The atmosphere was carnival, for the match they were supposed to have seen first was a men's doubles, with no disrespect to Jonas Bjorkman, Max Mirnyi, Alexander Waske and Rainer Schuettler.

The semi started briskly, as if both players were determined to shake off the stupor of having spent most of the

afternoon watching re-runs of Connors vs McEnroe from the early 1980s. In the previous five rounds, Mauresmo had yielded not one set and only 22 games.

In the sixth game, Davenport surrendered two double faults and lost her serve after a brutal baseline rally, Mauresmo held to love and was prepared

to win the set after just 25 minutes. It took another 25 minutes more, though, because Davenport has shown over the years a tendency to get stronger when stung rather than collapse in on herself.

She made Mauresmo feel uncomfortable enough to serve a double at set point and broke back. Not long ▶

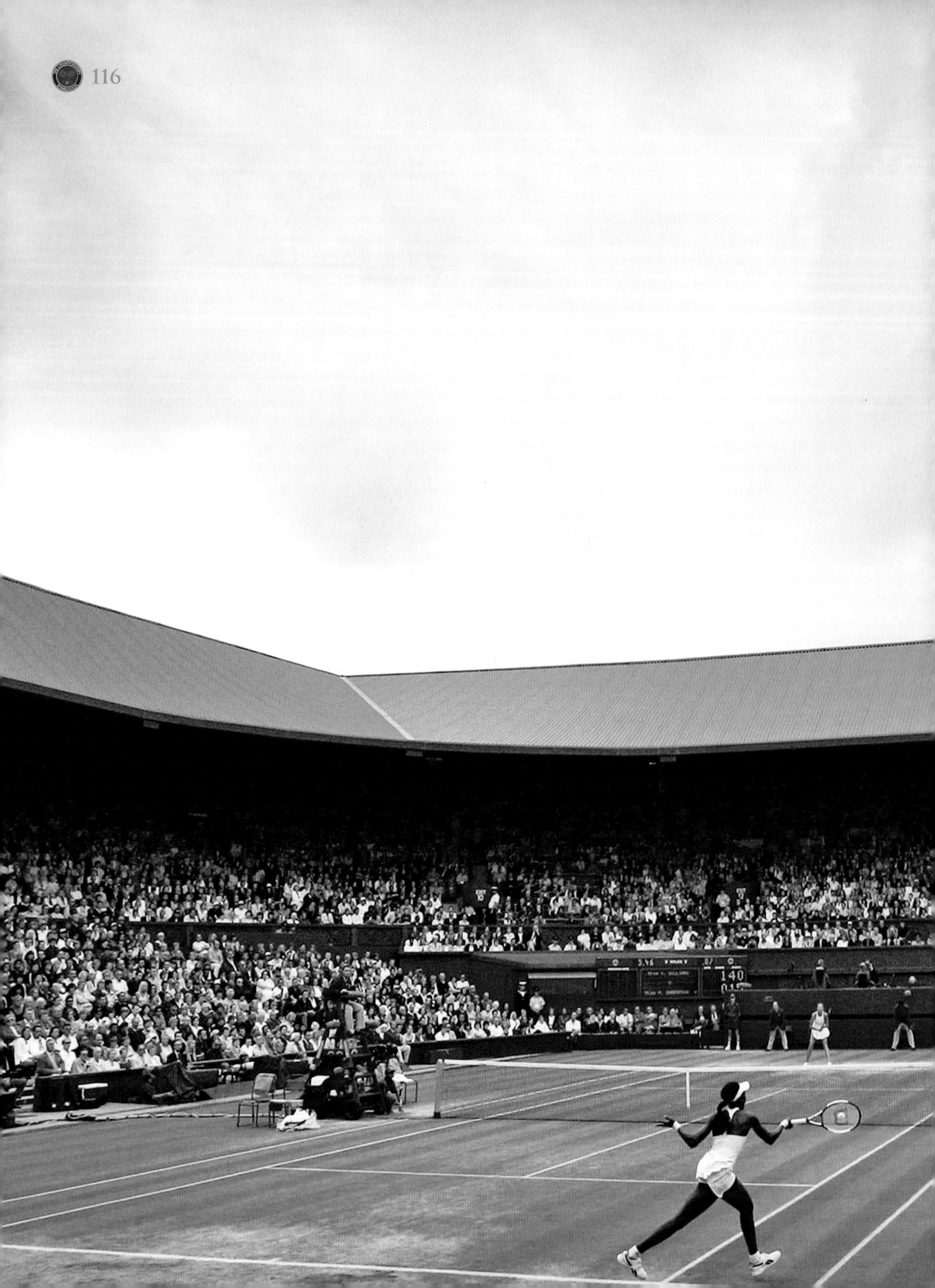

after, she had transformed the match, the French girl successively double-faulting, steering a volley wide, and slashing wildly at a backhand to leave the world No.1 serving for the set. But the drama of the set had not fully paid out, for Davenport made a pig's ear of her advantage, thrashing a smash way out and double-faulting. The set eventually went the French girl's way, after a tie-break, in which creativity off the ground kept company with white knuckle errors.

Mauresmo raced into a 3-1 lead in the second set. Surely she was on her way to a second grand slam final? There then followed a passage of play that was almost farcical, Mauresmo stumbling, Davenport breaking back, Davenport stumbling, Mauresmo breaking back, and so on and so forth into a second tie-break that Davenport clinched thanks to successive bludgeoning service winners on the eighth and ninth points.

The one break in the final set was Davenport's, by virtue of a netted backhand volley on the second opportunity, but as Mauresmo served at 3-5 down and won the opening point, the rains came again and the match was suspended, to return the following day with Davenport four points from a place in the final. ●

QUOTE
OF THE DAY

Venus Williams:
"I think many people have had this place [Centre Court]. Navratilova, Graf, Billie Jean King, all those people. It's just something that's rented, that's for sure."

DAY ELEVEN

1.7.05

FEDERER
vs
HEWITT

RODDICK
vs
JOHANSSON

DAVENPORT
vs
MAURESMO

FRIDAY, JULY 1

THE TREAT WAS SHORT LIVED – INDEED blink and it would have passed you by – but it was a treat nonetheless. Those patrons who had purchased tickets for Court No.1 on the second Friday of Wimbledon would have spent the intervening weeks preparing for a diet of over-35s, the prospect of seeing Martina Navratilova in unfettered flow, a spiky selection of doubles. Instead, they were offered the No.1 and No.3 players in the women's game.

Lindsay Davenport and Amelie Mauresmo had spent the previous night tossing and turning, wondering how they might play on their return after rain interrupted their semi-final with the No.1 leading the No.3 6-7, 7-6, 5-3 (0-15 on the Mauresmo serve). There may have been only four points required for Davenport to win, for Mauresmo, the French girl who had never won a grand slam after many heart-breaking near misses, was notoriously brittle.

But Mauresmo stood firm, and held the first three points. Davenport's reaction was pure assertion of her position; a love service game and a place in the final, brush your hands together, job done. "I have a lot of experience of matches being stopped but never when you are about to serve for a place in the Wimbledon final," Davenport said. "It was such a tough 24 hours. I was here at ten thirty yesterday warming up, we got onto the court around five thirty and got out of here at nine thirty. To come back in that situation was brutal. It was very mentally challenging to absorb all that was going on."

But that is the mark of a grand slam champion, to be able to absorb, to assimilate and, ultimately, to overcome. "This is so disappointing right now," Mauresmo said, "there is no way to rank the disappointment [of her four semi-final defeats]. It is just that I felt I was going to be able to win this match. I played good tennis, very aggressive throughout the match, whether serving or returning."

But Mauresmo was on her way again, a round too soon, not quite able to flourish when the need arose. Meanwhile Davenport would return for a third day in succession at the coalface.

Centre Court, there was no doubting when the patrons came to see, hosted a semi-final that was, to all intents and ranking purposes, the final. Whatever the stage of The Championships, it was fair to say that Roger Federer treated it as something very commonplace.

That is meant as absolutely no disrespect to Lleyton Hewitt, for the second-best player in the world played as well as the second-best player in the world could, and yet Federer won 6-3, 6-4, 7-6 and did not appear to have ▶

The grand slam dream dies once more for Amelie Mauresmo (left and far left), this time against Lindsay Davenport

Top: Referee Alan Mills prays for sun one last time

Andy Roddick follows through

Johansson's first service game was a case in point, because he sent down four aces and, on the one break point of the possible play on Friday, he came up with a service winner. In two further games, the Swedish 12th seed slapped forehands into the net to trail love-30, only to find something a bit extra to extricate himself from the trouble he had caused. Roddick led 6-5, on serve, when the groundstaff came hurtling on and the players disappeared.

There was no need for Federer to hurtle at all. A look at the respective records of the defending champion and Hewitt before they locked horns and there was not much to choose between them; No.1 and No.2 in the Indesit ATP Rankings, Federer leading in titles 29 to 24, his record at Wimbledon was 23-4 to Hewitt's 21-5, their grass court record this year was 10-0 and 8-1 and their entire career match record read Federer 370-122, Hewitt 393-116. The statistic most devoured, though, was the one that gave Federer a 9-8 overall head-to-head advantage and, since their meeting in the quarter-finals here last year, the Swiss had not dropped a set to Hewitt in four matches, including the US Open final last year, which he won 6-0, 7-6, 6-0.

That was the imposing standard that Hewitt somehow had to confront. And so, when he dropped his first service game, the portents were not enticing. Hewitt, to his credit, broke straight back, so perhaps Federer was churning a little beneath the flicks of his hair away from his bandanna, which suggests a studied nonchalance.

He won the first set on a 37 per cent first service percentage, which showed the extent to which he was able to dominate elsewhere. The second set was bagged the moment the Australian made five backhand errors in the fifth game to drop serve. Give him his due, Hewitt's resolve stiffened in the third, he was almost falling over himself staying in the rallies, he did all that he could, he scurried for all his worth and, actually, had a real chance at 6-5 when Federer wobbled seriously for the first time. At love-30, Hewitt could not have wished a second serve to bounce more welcomingly into his backhand hitting

broken a shirt-soaking sweat. Had Hewitt been able to extend himself, Federer would have extended himself that bit more, such is the understated genius of the 23-year-old from Basle.

The gods, and the schedulers, were on his side. More often than not, the match that is considered the more exciting of the two men's semi-finals was played second, for highly valued BBC tea-time consumption.

The reasoning behind Federer playing Hewitt first was that Australia might see a bit of their boy before they retired to bed. A bit was what they got. What happened? It was all over in a touch

over two hours, Andy Roddick and Thomas Johansson managed to play 11 games in 33 minutes and the drizzle became too hazardous to continue.

Federer did not need any helping hands, the favours could be saved for others but, I am sure, he was thankful anyway. Sleep came to him on Friday evening as easily as it always did, while Roddick, especially, may have spent less time on his computer playing online poker to all hours and, instead, working on how he might shake off Johansson upon Saturday's resumption.

There were opportunities aplenty for the American in the first set.

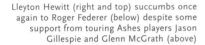
Lleyton Hewitt (right and top) succumbs once again to Roger Federer (below) despite some support from touring Ashes players Jason Gillespie and Glenn McGrath (above)

zone, but he knocked it too deep. Federer, reprieved, served two aces and you could see the blood drain from Hewitt's face. The tie break and match was gone when a tame netted backhand and a double fault put the Australian 4-1 down.

Simon Barnes in *The Times* said that Federer had caused the Centre Court crowd to add two sounds to its repertoire. "The first is a gasp of astonishment, an exhalation of complete wonder and disbelief," he wrote. "It means, basically, I am not seeing that. The second Federer-specific is a sigh of satisfaction, almost of repletion, an acknowledgement of the final, perfect shot, the sort of sound you make to yourself after a movement of the Goldberg Variations."

Hewitt put it a touch more prosaically: "The longer the match went, the better I felt I hit the ball. But he served better than me, he dictated play better than me. That's basically where he got the win. I've just got to bide my time, keep grinding away and look for answers. I feel as though my game has improved in the last 18 months, I'm definitely the second-best player going around at the moment. It's just that the best player going around is pretty bloody good." ●

QUOTE
OF THE DAY

Roger Federer:

*"It's important to respect each
other. He didn't have too much
to cheer about today, so he's not
going to scream when he holds
his serve because that's a normal
thing in tennis. I think if he's up
two sets to love, he's going to be
screaming enough. Have to
enjoy this while he's not."*

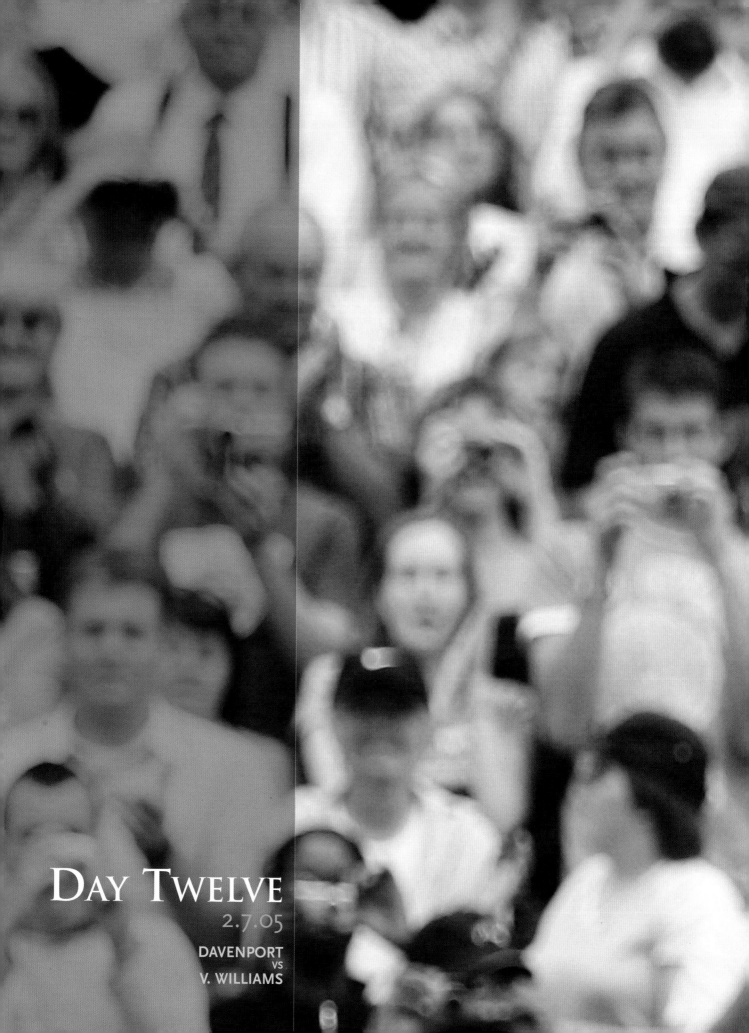

Day Twelve

2.7.05

DAVENPORT
vs
V. WILLIAMS

Saturday,
July 2

OF THE MANY MUSINGS ABOUT WIMBLEDON
2005 one from a leading United States
commentator struck me as a particularly
vivid thought for the ladies' final.
"Venus needs a new coach, Venus
needs to remodel her forehand, Venus
is vulnerable to pressure on her second
serve, Venus has lost interest, Venus has
never recovered from surrendering [her
supremacy] to Serena... raise your right
hand if you're not standing in the buffet
line for humble pie right now."

As we watched Venus Williams
cavorting across Centre Court in the
aftermath of her 4-6, 7-6, 9-7 victory
over Lindsay Davenport in the final,
all of those recent indulgences when

commentating on the state of her game
came back to one's mind. There was not
one person in the audience and certainly
on the press benches, who had not raised
one of those concerns in four years since
she last clinched a grand slam title.

But rewind a bit. Though it had been
a while since either had won a major –
Davenport's trophy-less streak went back
to the 2000 Australian Open – they had
held the No.1 ranking for 86 weeks
between them, earned over $35 million
in official prize money and claimed 79
titles on the tour, including an Olympic
gold medal each. Hardly duff finalists.

Williams had defeated the defending
champion, Maria Sharapova, in the

QUOTE
OF THE DAY

Lindsay Davenport:
"I don't feel I have all that to be ashamed of. I'm really disappointed, obviously you would be when you get so close to winning Wimbledon and it doesn't happen. But someone deserves it more than I do, and someone can come up with those shots. She was able to come up with [shots] at those times, I don't know what to say. It's too good. She deserved it."

semi-finals, Davenport had staged a brilliant recovery to edge Amelie Mauresmo. Totalling how long they had spent on court in their six previous matches, Williams had done 20 minutes more, and as for their average time spent completing matches, Williams needed four minutes more to win. Davenport had played 20 games more.

It was to become as memorably close as those figures portended. Williams, asked to serve first, started in the manner of the car whose initials are the same as hers. From the moment the engine clicked over, she was purring. But then she scrunched her first change of gears. A couple of double faults in the third game and an errant backhand, offered Davenport a lead she enhanced by breaking again in the seventh game,

Lindsay's trials: Davenport
remonstrates with the umpire
and then (below) receives
treatment on her back

Right: The two finalists embrace

when Williams made a couple of
mistakes on her forehand wing.

Then, suddenly, Williams reeled off
nine points in succession, a stream of
winners brought to a halt by a netted
backhand that gave Davenport the head
of steam she required to see the first set
through after 33 minutes. Davenport
staved off a break point in the fourth
game of the second set, Williams two
in the following game, Davenport saved
a set point in the tenth game when
Williams struck a service return from
a second serve a foot too long. Then
came the first real moment of truth.

In a flash, at 5-5, Williams was 0-40
down on her serve, aided by one dire
double fault and a netted backhand.
Davenport missed one chance when
she nudged a backhand wide but on

the second, with Venus having slipped over on a green patch and able to make only token contact, the break was Davenport's. She would stride out to serve for the match.

Williams sensed she could not afford to stay back, so she headed forward to put away a forehand volley, struck a decisive backhand right into the corner and pulverised another backhand winner. Davenport, unnerved, erred on her backhand and, in a flash, had lost serve to love.

Having stepped up a stride, Venus could not back off and led 5-1 in the tie-break, only to become momentarily unsettled and, at 5-2, lose two points on her serve, with Davenport needing to hold the next to bring it all-square. Instead, rushing a touch, she netted a backhand, offering the incentive that her opponent did not reject, punching home a glorious forehand to square the match.

If the first two sets drained most viewers, the third was to leave them breathless. Davenport broke first, as she had done in sets one and two, to lead 4-2. At 40-15, she delivered what she believed was an ace down the "T", only for it to be called wide and, in the midst of throwing herself into the action and recoiling, felt something give in her back. Davenport then served a double fault, a forehand volley by Williams landed right on the chalk and the No.1, now clearly struggling, made two backhand errors to lose her initiative.

The trainer was called for, Davenport was manipulated for a couple of minutes on the court and then disappeared from view for further treatment. It was 4-4. In the players' box, Richard Williams was brushing both his hair and his beard, obviously preparing for what he felt would be his daughter's coronation. But some of the aches had been soothed from Davenport and at 5-4, 30-all, Venus served a double fault. Championship point to Davenport. It is usual for the ▶

Three-times Wimbledon Champion Venus Williams lifts the winner's plate (right), even if she can't quite believe how she came through the marathon third set (left)

Back in the high life again: Venus holds the famous plate for a third time

player match-point down to try to stay in the rally, hoping that the opponent attempts to go for a winner too soon, but Williams, to her credit, seized on a short ball and drove a backhand winner down Davenport's forehand wing. It was the only time Davenport was to be that close.

The tempo did not drop, if anything it picked up. Rallies were long and punishing but eventually, having saved two break points in the 15th game, a crosscourt forehand winner from Williams gave her the lead for the first time in the set and, though she double faulted on her first match point, a forehand error from Davenport and the longest Wimbledon women's final was won.

Williams could not contain herself, indeed had the roof been installed, she would have leapt through it, so heady was her celebration. I don't think HRH The Duke of Kent, the president of the

All England Club, had ever been curtseyed to so often in 20 seconds. Venus was in orbit.

I found her father tucking into a bowl of pasta and cranberry sauce less than an hour after the match. Had they had much chance to speak? "I have just told her," he said, "if I was her I would look to be No.1 again. She needs to work on her technique, on her movement, to go down the T more with her serve, to play her forehand down the line rather than crosscourt and if she works on those, when she comes to the US Open, [Maria] Sharapova will be there and Venus can whip her again, Lindsay will be there and she can get her. You don't want to win just this time so it becomes a fluke, get your technique together and be ready to roll."

Richard confessed how close he was to tears to see Venus enjoying the moment of victory, reminded of how she used to bound around as a child who never stayed still for a minute. And it was the ideology their father instilled that helped see his children through the times when

no-one believed in them but family. "We were never allowed to say 'can't' at all at our house," Venus said. "We weren't allowed to be negative."

"The most annoying part [of the criticism of her] was the fact that when you're playing your best, doing your best, so many people want to be on your side but if things get a little... or you don't win every match, there's so many people who want to put you down. So many people who thrive on negativity, so many people who are excited to see a story like that. That's the part I was disappointed in, because I don't think that is the only way it has to be because that's not how I was raised."

It had been almost forgotten that, earlier in the day on Centre Court, Andy Roddick had secured victory over Thomas Johansson of Sweden, 6-7, 6-2, 7-6, 7-6, to earn his place in a second consecutive Wimbledon final and that, as evening descended, the great Martina Navratilova, trying to win her record 21st title at the club, had been beaten in the semi-finals of both the ladies and mixed doubles. Perhaps this was one fairy-tale comeback that was not meant to be. ●

Once more into the breach: Andy Roddick (left and above) powers through to a second Wimbledon final

DAY THIRTEEN
3.7.05

FEDERER
VS
RODDICK

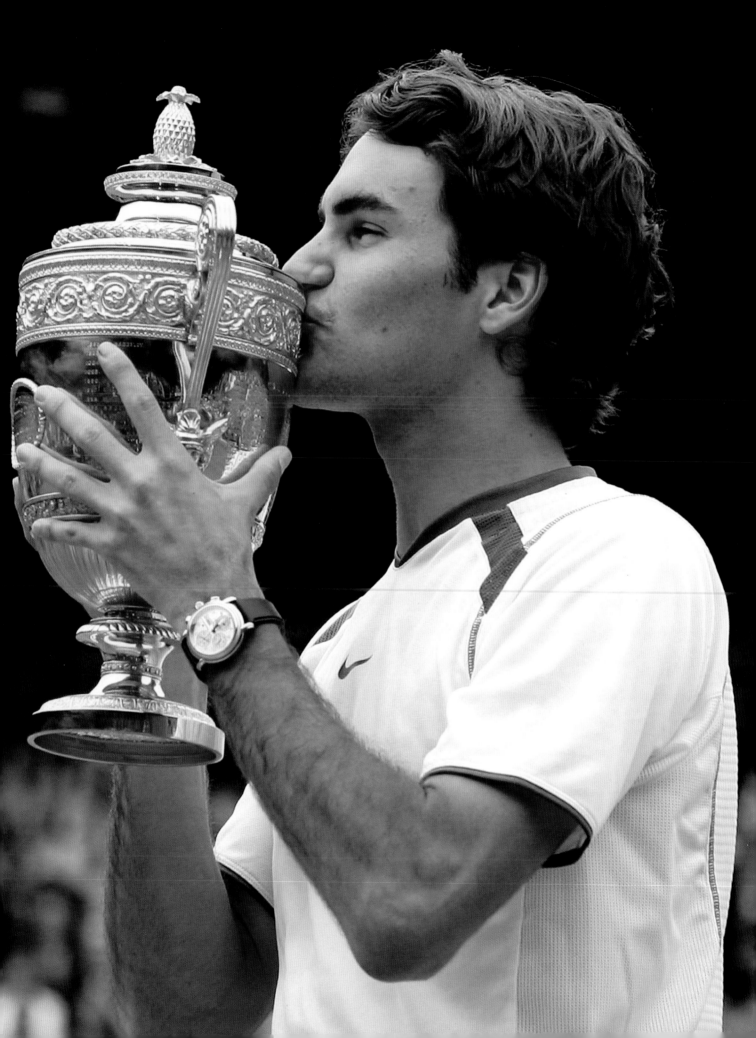

SUNDAY, JULY 3

WIMBLEDON 2005 WAS THE 119TH STAGING of The Lawn Tennis Championships, which began in 1877 with Spencer Gore defeating William Marshall 6-1, 6-2, 6-4 for the inaugural title. This was the 38th staging of The Championships in the Open Era that started in 1968 with Australia's Rod Laver defeating countryman Tony Roche 6-3, 6-4, 6-2 in the final.

If that seems a long-winded way of getting around to Roger Federer against Andy Roddick, it struck me that there was a fascinating link with the history lesson at the top. Roche was on Centre Court again, seated in the players' box, a man who had never won a Wimbledon final, who had been unable to coach three players, Chris Lewis of New Zealand, Ivan Lendl of Czechoslovakia, or Pat Rafter of Australia to the crown – indeed, they all lost in the final themselves – and was back on another last Sunday in what must have seemed like the most comfortable position in the place.

In November, 2004, Roche received one of those phone calls anyone would yearn for. On the end of the line was Federer, without a doubt the best player in the world, asking for a bit of help to stay there. Could he, for instance, spend some time at Roche's home in New South Wales during Christmas and could they possibly team up a few times during the following year to make sure Federer stayed a step ahead. What does one say? No?

Not everything had gone according to plan in Australia and France; Federer had been defeated in two semi-finals and both were crushing blows. But he had targeted the grass as the event he really wanted to win and now he was in the final, having won five of his previous six rounds in straight sets, and was again faced with the young American who wanted this above all titles to add to his 2003 US Open triumph.

Primal scream: Andy Roddick's passion wasn't enough to overcome Federer's mastery

Left: paralympian Peter Norfolk MBE oversaw the toss

Roger Federer's power and poise floored brave challenger Andy Roddick (right) for a second consecutive year

Roddick was more powerful; he had worked hard on his fitness, he looked leaner and meaner, his game had more elements to it that he had hoped would concern Federer, though this was their tenth meeting and the Swiss had won eight of the previous nine, the last three in finals. And, speaking of finals, Federer had won 20 of those in succession as well. Armed with those statistics, Roddick did well to show at all.

Peter Norfolk, MBE, the British gold medallist at the Quad Singles at the 2004 Athens Paralympics, presided over the toss of the coin, which Federer won and chose to serve. The first game of the final was a statement in capital letters. I'M READY. He did not make an error, but then Roddick did the same, holding to love. There was only one point against serve in the first five games before Federer struck, whacking a forehand winner when Roddick could not quite lace a smash, and a driven service return forced a clumsy forehand from his opponent. For a moment it looked like the No.2 seed was in danger of being demoralised, especially when he dropped the set in 21 minutes.

Roddick broke him once, in the third game of the second set, but was broken back in the sixth. The American did not win a point on his serve in the second set tie-break and when they emerged after a 25-minute delay for drizzle, the single break in the third set went, of course, to Federer. His 6-2, 7-6, 6-4 victory was an historic third in a row, joining only two others, Bjorn Borg and Pete Sampras to accomplish the task in the Open Era.

He said at the end that it was "a pity" for his opponent that he had played so well. Roddick – whose "aaarghs" and "cummmns" (he doesn't do the full frontal "c'monnn" like Lleyton Hewitt but mutters it beneath his breath) are the sounds likely to be most closely associated with the 2005 final – would not want to be pitied. He accepts that when he steps out, this is where he wants to be, these are the arenas he loves, and more often than not, he would be the victor.

Playing Federer is something different, especially when the champion is in such an imperious mood. This, he said, was the greatest performance of his life. "I remember during the match and

thinking during the rain delay, I didn't even feel as if I was really playing, it was so strange," he said.

There was a point when Federer made a startling mishit – he puts so much on every ball that these things happen – and managed to turn that to his advantage. It was as if he had deliberately set his opponent up with a shot off the frame, but that is the illusion he creates. This kind of perfection is mesmerising rather than exciting and it certainly mesmerised Roddick. By the end, he must have felt like a man fighting a ghost. Roddick said: "He is as close as there is to unbeatable. I felt I played decent, the stats are decent and I got straight-setted. I'm going to continue to work hard, I'm not going to sulk and cry, I tried playing different ways, I tried to go to his forehand and came in, and he passed me and I tried the same to his backhand and he passed me. It's not as if I have a lot of questions leaving the court. I was trying different things. I hoped he gets bored or something."

Tedium is not a prospect that sits too well with the champion. Nor does anyone else wish he falls out of love with capturing the major silverware, ▶

QUOTE
OF THE DAY

Andy Roddick:

"I just said 'Congratulations'. There's not much more you can say. I have loads of respect for him as a person as well. I've told him before 'I'd love to hate you, but you're really nice'."

Q: *You said you have to tip your hat to him. Are you able to do that during the heat of a game?*
A: *No, I'm in denial the whole time I'm out there. Listen, I still want a crack at him until my record is 1-31. He's the measuring stick to know where you are and where you need to go.*

except one or two of the opposition. He cannot actually say he did not think they are likely to be able to challenge him for a while, even if he suspected it. He is too nice a guy.

As is Roche. And Federer had a special word for him the following day. "I'm really happy our partnership has worked out," he said. "I felt as if he was carried away a bit, too. We reflected on that at the Champions' Dinner last night. It was a really nice occasion."

Indeed, as ever, the Savoy Hotel was a gracious host, as the great and good joined together to savour one of the very finest of Wimbledon fortnights. There were a few new faces in the gathering as well. Who would have said when Stephen Huss of Australia and Wesley Moodie of South Africa teamed up to try to get through the qualifying – they had previously won an ATP challenger in far off New Caledonia and that was it – that they would emerge as the men's doubles champions?

Just champion: Roger Federer
marks the winning moment

In the final, they defeated Bob and Mike Bryan – appearing in their third grand slam final of the year – 7-6, 6-3, 6-7, 6-3. What irony that at the end of a week when Todd Woodbridge, perhaps the finest doubles player ever, should have retired from tennis, a comparative unknown in Huss, should have replaced him as Wimbledon champion.

Cara Black, a two-time doubles champion in 2004, had to restrict herself to one event this time around, partnering Liezel Huber of South Africa, the No.2 seeds, to a 6-2, 6-1 victory over the scratch pair of Svetlana Kuznetsova and Amelie Mauresmo. How good, though, to see Mauresmo in a grand slam final and enjoying it so much.

Mahesh Bhupathi became a Wimbledon champion for the third time with a third different partner. In 1999, he had won the men's doubles with his Indian compatriot, Leander Paes, three years later he was a mixed champion with Russia's Elena

Likhovtseva and in 2005, Mary Pierce of France partnered him to victory. It was Pierce's first title in SW19.

Jeremy Chardy from Pau, in France, a tall, dark, handsome teenager, became the boys' singles champion, defeating Robin Haase of The Netherlands (a bit too much of a Richard Krajicek lookalike for comfort) 6-4, 6-3. The girls' singles crown went to Agnieszka Radwanska of Poland, who beat Tamira Paszek of Austria, 6-3, 6-4.

In the boys' doubles, Andrew Kennaugh of Great Britain and Samuel Groth of Australia had won their semi-final 15-13, completing it on the morning of the final, and so it was no real surprise that they should fall 6-4, 6-1 to American pair Jesse Levine and Michael Shabaz.

The cream rose to the top in the girls' doubles with the No.1 seeded pair of Viktoria Azarenko of Belarus and Agnes Szavay of Hungary defeating second seeds Marina Erakovic of New Zealand

and Monica Niculescu of Romania 7-6, 2-6, 6-0.

It was wonderful to see old faces again – even if many of them had not aged a bit. Ellis Ferreira of South Africa teamed with Paul Haarhuis (is he really over 35?) to win the over-35s doubles. They were a mite too young for the American pair TJ Middleton and David Wheaton 6-3, 6-4. Tracy Austin broke away from her commentating duties for both the BBC and NBC to team with Jana Novotna, the 1998 singles champion, to lift the ladies' over-35s doubles title with a 6-2, 6-4 win over Katrina Adams of the USA and Rosalyn Fairbank-Nideffer of South Africa.

Completing The Championship line up in the over-45s doubles, Kevin Curren and Johan Kriek from South Africa defeated the Aussie Macs, Peter McNamara and Paul McNamee 6-4, 3-6, 7-6. I reported on all four of those in my first Wimbledon, but I'm not telling what year that was!

▶

THE GENTLEMEN'S SINGLES CHAMPIONSHIP
ROGER FEDERER

THE LADIES' SINGLES CHAMPIONSHIP
VENUS WILLIAMS

THE GENTLEMEN'S DOUBLES CHAMPIONSHIP
STEPHEN HUSS & WESLEY MOODIE

THE LADIES DOUBLES CHAMPIONSHIP
CARA BLACK & LIEZEL HUBER

THE MIXED DOUBLES CHAMPIONSHIP
MAHESH BHUPATHI & MARY PIERCE

THE GENTLEMEN'S WHEELCHAIR DOUBLES CHAMPIONSHIP
MICHAEL JEREMIASZ & JAYANT MISTRY

THE BOYS' SINGLES CHAMPIONSHIP
JEREMY CHARDY

THE GIRLS' SINGLES CHAMPIONSHIP
AGNIESZKA RADWANSKA

THE BOYS' DOUBLES CHAMPIONSHIP
JESSE LEVINE & MICHAEL SHABAZ

THE GIRLS' DOUBLES CHAMPIONSHIP
VIKTORIA AZARENKA & AGNES SZAVAY

THE 35 & OVER GENTLEMEN'S DOUBLES CHAMPIONSHIP
ELLIS FERREIRA & PAUL HAARHUIS

THE 45 & OVER GENTLEMEN'S DOUBLES CHAMPIONSHIP
KEVIN CURREN & JOHAN KRIEK

CHAMPIONSHIP
RECORDS
2005

ALPHABETICAL LIST OF COMPETITORS

LADIES

20 Arvidsson Miss S. *(Sweden)*
24 Asagoe Miss S. *(Japan)*
61 Baltacha Miss E. *(Great Britain)*
89 Bartoli Miss M. *(France)*
100 Beltrame Miss S. *(France)*
63 Benesova Miss I. *(Czech Republic)*
Beygelzimer Miss Y. *(Ukraine)*
82 Birnerova Miss E. *(Czech Republic)*
102 Black Miss C. *(Zimbabwe)*
50 Bohmova Miss K. *(Czech Republic)*
119 Bondarenko Miss A. *(Ukraine)*
108 Bondarenko Miss K. *(Ukraine)*
37 Borwell Miss S. *(Great Britain)*
106 Brandi Miss K. *(Puerto Rico)*
22 Callens Miss E.S.H. *(Belgium)*
114 Camerin Miss M. *(Italy)*
103 Castano Miss C. *(Colombia)*
84 Cervanova Miss L. *(Slovakia)*
55 Chakvetadze Miss A. *(Russia)*
75 Chladkova Miss D. *(Czech Republic)*
123 Cho Miss Y.J. *(South Korea)*
16 Clijsters Miss K. *(Belgium)*
Cohen-Aloro Miss S. *(France)*
92 Craybas Miss J. *(USA)*
Curran Miss C. *(Great Britain)*
34 Czink Miss M. *(Hungary)*
66 Daniilidou Miss E. *(Greece)*
1 Davenport Miss L. *(USA)*
113 Dechy Miss N. *(France)*
64 Dementieva Miss E. *(Russia)*
53 Diaz-Oliva Miss M. *(Argentina)*
36 Domachowska Miss M. *(Poland)*
51 Dominikovic Miss E. *(Australia)*
74 Douchevina Miss V. *(Russia)*
69 Dulko Miss G. *(Argentina)*
41 Farina Elia Mrs S. *(Italy)*
70 Fedak Miss J. *(Ukraine)*
76 Foretz Miss S. *(France)*
57 Frazier Miss A. *(USA)*
90 Fujiwara Miss R. *(Japan)*
71 Gagliardi Miss E. *(Switzerland)*
Gallovits Miss E. *(Romania)*
78 Garbin Miss T. *(Italy)*
120 Golovin Miss T. *(France)*
Grandin Miss N. *(South Africa)*
68 Granville Miss L. *(USA)*
116 Groenefeld Miss A-L. *(Germany)*
88 Hantuchova Miss D. *(Slovakia)*
91 Harkleroad Miss A. *(USA)*
Hawkins Miss A. *(Great Britain)*
95 Haynes Miss A. *(USA)*
65 Henin-Hardenne Mrs J. *(Belgium)*
Hopkins Miss J. *(USA)*
Huber Mrs L. *(South Africa)*
Husarova Miss J. *(Slovakia)*
13 Irvin Miss M. *(USA)*
73 Ivanovic Miss A. *(Serbia and Montenegro)*
4 Jackson Miss J. *(USA)*
125 Janes Miss A. *(Great Britain)*
56 Jankovic Miss J. *(Serbia and Montenegro)*
2 Jidkova Miss A. *(Russia)*
126 Karatantcheva Miss S. *(Bulgaria)*
54 Keothavong Miss A. *(Great Britain)*
21 Kirilenko Miss M. *(Russia)*
62 Klaschka Miss S. *(Germany)*
26 Kostanic Miss J. *(Croatia)*
67 Koukalova Miss K. *(Czech Republic)*
Krauth Miss E. *(Argentina)*
12 Kremer Miss A. *(Luxembourg)*
Krizan Miss T. *(Slovenia)*
32 Kuznetsova Miss S. *(Russia)*
Lee Miss J. *(Chinese Taipei)*
48 Likhovtseva Miss E. *(Russia)*
87 Linetskaya Miss E. *(Russia)*
127 Llagostera Vives Miss N. *(Spain)*
31 Llewellyn Miss R. *(Great Britain)*
60 Loit Miss E. *(France)*
23 Maleeva Miss M. *(Bulgaria)*
7 Mamic Miss S. *(Croatia)*
3 Marrero Miss M. *(Spain)*
107 Martinez Miss C. *(Spain)*
33 Mauresmo Miss A. *(France)*
McShea Miss L. *(Australia)*
121 Medina Garrigues Miss A. *(Spain)*
30 Mirza Miss S. *(India)*
Miyagi Miss N. *(Japan)*
Morariu Miss C. *(USA)*
29 Morigami Miss A. *(Japan)*
Musgrave Miss T. *(Australia)*
49 Myskina Miss A. *(Russia)*
52 Nakamura Miss A. *(Japan)*
Navratilova Miss G. *(Czech Republic)*
Navratilova Miss M. *(USA)*
15 O'Brien Miss K. *(Great Britain)*
115 O'Donoghue Miss J. *(Great Britain)*
14 Obata Miss S. *(Japan)*
101 Ondraskova Miss Z. *(Czech Republic)*
6 Osterloh Miss L. *(USA)*
117 Panova Miss T. *(Russia)*
124 Parra Santonja Miss A. *(Spain)*
28 Pastikova Miss M. *(Czech Republic)*
86 Peer Miss S. *(Israel)*
Pelletier Miss M. *(Canada)*
72 Pennetta Miss F. *(Italy)*
19 Perebiynis Miss T. *(Ukraine)*
38 Perry Miss S. *(USA)*
109 Peschke Miss K. *(Czech Republic)*
97 Petrova Miss N. *(Russia)*
80 Pierce Miss M. *(France)*
94 Poutchek Miss T. *(Belarussia)*
83 Pratt Miss N.J. *(Australia)*
110 Randriantefy Miss D. *(Madagascar)*
118 Raymond Miss L.M. *(USA)*
104 Razzano Miss V. *(France)*
Rodionova Miss A. *(Russia)*
98 Ruano Pascual Miss V. *(Spain)*
Russell Miss J. *(USA)*
79 Safarova Miss L. *(Czech Republic)*
8 Safina Miss D. *(Russia)*
35 Sanchez Lorenzo Miss M. *(Spain)*
93 Santangelo Miss M. *(Italy)*
99 Schaul Miss C. *(Luxembourg)*
105 Schiavone Miss F. *(Italy)*
17 Schnyder Miss P. *(Switzerland)*
46 Schruff Miss J. *(Germany)*
44 Sequera Miss M. *(Venezuela)*
18 Serra Zanetti Miss A. *(Italy)*
59 Sfar Miss S. *(Tunisia)*
128 Sharapova Miss M. *(Russia)*
45 Shaughnessy Miss M. *(USA)*
47 Smashnova Miss A. *(Israel)*
South Miss M. *(Great Britain)*
11 Spears Miss A. *(USA)*
40 Sprem Miss K. *(Croatia)*
122 Srebotnik Miss K. *(Slovenia)*
Stewart Miss B. *(Australia)*
27 Stosur Miss S. *(Australia)*
5 Strycova Miss B. *(Czech Republic)*
Stubbs Miss R.P. *(Australia)*
42 Sucha Miss M. *(Slovakia)*
9 Sugiyama Miss A. *(Japan)*
Talaja Miss S. *(Croatia)*
39 Tanasugarn Miss T. *(Thailand)*
85 Tu Miss M. *(USA)*
25 Vaidisova Miss N. *(Czech Republic)*
77 Vakulenko Miss J. *(Ukraine)*
Vanc Miss A. *(Romania)*
43 Vento-Kabchi Mrs M. *(Venezuela)*
10 Vinci Miss R. *(Italy)*
Voskoboeva Miss G. *(Russia)*
58 Washington Miss M. *(USA)*
Webley-Smith Miss E. *(Great Britain)*
111 Weingartner Miss M. *(Germany)*
96 Williams Miss S. *(USA)*
81 Williams Miss V. *(USA)*
Yakimova Miss A. *(Belarussia)*
112 Zvonareva Miss V. *(Russia)*

GENTLEMEN

21 Acasuso J. *(Argentina)*
Allegro Y. *(Switzerland)*
99 Almagro N. *(Spain)*
49 Ancic M. *(Croatia)*
122 Andreev I. *(Russia)*
Arnold L. *(Argentina)*
103 Arthurs W. *(Australia)*
Artoni E. *(Italy)*
Aspelin S. *(Sweden)*
Auckland J. *(Great Britain)*
Bachelot J-F. *(France)*
26 Baghdatis M. *(Cyprus)*
Banks A. *(Great Britain)*
Barker R. *(Great Britain)*
Barker W. *(Great Britain)*
84 Bastl G. *(Switzerland)*
61 Beck K. *(Slovakia)*
114 Behrend T. *(Germany)*
7 Benneteau J. *(France)*
46 Berdych T. *(Czech Republic)*
Bertolini M. *(Italy)*
Bhupathi M. *(India)*
29 Bjorkman J. *(Sweden)*
Black W. *(Zimbabwe)*
36 Blake J. *(USA)*
44 Bogdanovic A. *(Great Britain)*
125 Bracciali D. *(Italy)*
Bryan B. *(USA)*
Bryan M. *(USA)*
47 Burgsmuller L. *(Germany)*
117 Calatrava A. *(Spain)*
110 Carlsen K. *(Denmark)*
Cermak F. *(Czech Republic)*
Cibulec T. *(Czech Republic)*
76 Clement A. *(France)*
Coetzee J. *(South Africa)*
113 Coria G. *(Argentina)*
Damm M. *(Czech Republic)*
32 Davydenko N. *(Russia)*
10 Delgado J. *(Great Britain)*
Delgado R. *(Paraguay)*
41 Dent T. *(USA)*
6 Di Mauro A. *(Italy)*
108 Djokovic N. *(Serbia and Montenegro)*
31 Draper S. *(Australia)*
45 Dupuis A. *(France)*
91 Elseneer G. *(Belgium)*
11 Enqvist T. *(Sweden)*
Erlich J. *(Israel)*
Etlis G. *(Argentina)*
1 Federer R. *(Switzerland)*
105 Ferrer D. *(Spain)*
9 Ferrero J.C. *(Spain)*
Fisher A. *(Australia)*
Friedl L. *(Czech Republic)*
Fyrstenberg M. *(Poland)*
Galimberti G. *(Italy)*
38 Garcia A. *(Chile)*
Garcia M. *(Argentina)*
106 Garcia-Lopez G. *(Spain)*
89 Gasquet R. *(France)*
37 Gimelstob J. *(USA)*
82 Ginepri R. *(USA)*
66 Goldstein P. *(USA)*
24 Gonzalez F. *(Chile)*
5 Goodall J. *(Great Britain)*
112 Grosjean S. *(France)*
73 Haas T. *(Germany)*
102 Haehnel J. *(France)*
Haggard C. *(South Africa)*
109 Hanescu V. *(Romania)*
Hanley P. *(Australia)*
97 Henman T. *(Great Britain)*
27 Hernandez O. *(Spain)*
35 Hernych J. *(Czech Republic)*
33 Hewitt L. *(Australia)*
Hilton M. *(Great Britain)*
Hood M. *(Argentina)*
86 Horna L. *(Peru)*
56 Hrbaty D. *(Slovakia)*
Huss S. *(Australia)*
17 Johansson J. *(Sweden)*
80 Johansson T. *(Sweden)*
78 Karanusic R. *(Croatia)*
126 Karlovic I. *(Croatia)*
Kerr J. *(Australia)*
118 Ketola T. *(Finland)*
8 Kiefer N. *(Germany)*
Kiernan D. *(Great Britain)*
43 Kim K. *(USA)*
Knowle J. *(Austria)*
Knowles M. *(Bahamas)*
Koenig R. *(South Africa)*
Kohlmann M. *(Germany)*
90 Kohlschreiber P. *(Germany)*
52 Koubek S. *(Austria)*
85 Kucera K. *(Slovakia)*
Landsberg J. *(Sweden)*
Leach R. *(USA)*
12 Lee H-T. *(South Korea)*
Levinsky J. *(Czech Republic)*
Lindstedt R. *(Sweden)*
28 Lisnard J-R. *(France)*
120 Ljubicic I. *(Croatia)*
111 Llodra M. *(France)*
57 Lopez F. *(Spain)*
Lopez Moron A. *(Spain)*
75 Lu Y-H. *(Chinese Taipei)*
23 Mackin A.R. *(Great Britain)*
MacPhie B. *(USA)*
Mahut N. *(France)*
116 Malisse X. *(Belgium)*
93 Mantilla F. *(Spain)*
115 Marray J. *(Great Britain)*
19 Martin A. *(Spain)*
40 Massu N. *(Chile)*
2 Mathieu P-H. *(France)*
Matkowski M. *(Poland)*
13 Mayer F. *(Germany)*
60 Mello R. *(Brazil)*
119 Melzer J. *(Austria)*
Mertinak M. *(Slovakia)*
3 Minar I. *(Czech Republic)*
67 Mirnyi M. *(Belarussia)*
107 Monaco J. *(Argentina)*
53 Monfils G. *(France)*
18 Montanes A. *(Spain)*
Moodie W. *(South Africa)*
30 Morrison J. *(USA)*
94 Muller G. *(Luxembourg)*
83 Murray A. *(Great Britain)*
96 Nadal R. *(Spain)*
88 Nalbandian D. *(Argentina)*
Niemeyer F. *(Canada)*
98 Nieminen J. *(Finland)*
42 Norman D. *(Belgium)*
72 Novak J. *(Czech Republic)*
54 Okun N. *(Israel)*
Oliver G. *(USA)*
Paes L. *(India)*
Pala P. *(Czech Republic)*
Palmer J. *(USA)*
Parmar A. *(Great Britain)*
Parrott T. *(USA)*
77 Pavel A. *(Romania)*
Perry T. *(Australia)*
Peya A. *(Austria)*
58 Phau B. *(Germany)*
62 Philippoussis M. *(Australia)*
101 Popp A. *(Germany)*
Prieto S. *(Argentina)*
48 Puerta M. *(Argentina)*
Ram A. *(Israel)*
Rikl D. *(Czech Republic)*
16 Robredo T. *(Spain)*
34 Rochus C. *(Belgium)*
65 Rochus O. *(Belgium)*
128 Roddick A. *(USA)*
Rodriguez M. *(Argentina)*
20 Rusedski G. *(Great Britain)*
Sa A. *(Brazil)*
64 Safin M. *(Russia)*
123 Sanguinetti D. *(Italy)*
70 Santoro F. *(France)*
39 Sargsian S. *(Armenia)*
55 Saulnier C. *(France)*
68 Schuettler R. *(Germany)*
124 Seppi A. *(Italy)*
59 Sherwood D. *(Great Britain)*
87 Sluiter R. *(Netherlands)*
121 Soderling R. *(Sweden)*
95 Spadea V. *(USA)*
63 Srichaphan P. *(Thailand)*
92 Starace P. *(Italy)*
81 Stepanek R. *(Czech Republic)*
Suk C. *(Czech Republic)*
50 Summerer T. *(Germany)*
4 Tabara M. *(Czech Republic)*
Thomas J. *(USA)*
74 Tipsarevic J. *(Serbia and Montenegro)*
100 Tursunov D. *(Russia)*
51 Udomchoke D. *(Thailand)*
79 Ulihrach B. *(Czech Republic)*
Ullyett K. *(Zimbabwe)*
127 Vanek J. *(Czech Republic)*
Vanhoudt T. *(Belgium)*
14 Ventura S. *(Spain)*
15 Verdasco F. *(Spain)*
Vico U. *(Italy)*
Vizner P. *(Czech Republic)*
104 Volandri F. *(Italy)*
Waske A. *(Germany)*
Wassen R. *(Netherlands)*
69 Wawrinka S. *(Switzerland)*
71 Wessels P. *(Netherlands)*
Woodbridge T.A. *(Australia)*
25 Youzhny M. *(Russia)*
22 Zib T. *(Czech Republic)*
Zimonjic N. *(Serbia and Montenegro)*

GIRLS

Alvarez Miss M-F. *(Bolivia)*
Azarenka Miss V. *(Belarussia)*
Aziz Miss M. *(Egypt)*
Besser Miss A. *(Italy)*
Buzarnescu Miss M. *(Romania)*
Chan Miss Y-J. *(Chinese Taipei)*
Cibulkova Miss D. *(Slovakia)*
Cohen Miss J. *(USA)*
Curtis Miss J. *(Great Britain)*
Erakovic Miss M. *(New Zealand)*
Errani Miss S. *(Italy)*
Frankova Miss N. *(Czech Republic)*
Gajdosova Miss J. *(Slovakia)*
Glatch Miss A. *(USA)*
Gojnea Miss M. *(Romania)*
Govortsova Miss O. *(Belarussia)*
Heinser Miss J-L. *(USA)*
King Miss V. *(USA)*
Kirkland Miss J. *(USA)*
Kleybanova Miss A. *(Russia)*
Kosminskaya Miss E. *(Russia)*
Kramperova Miss K. *(Czech Republic)*
Kudryavtseva Miss A. *(Russia)*
Lukaszewicz Miss O. *(Australia)*
Makarova Miss E. *(Russia)*
Molinero Miss F. *(Argentina)*
Morita Miss A. *(Japan)*
Niculescu Miss M. *(Romania)*
Olaru Miss R. *(Romania)*
Paszek Miss T. *(Austria)*
Pavlovic Miss I. *(France)*
Peterzan Miss C. *(Great Britain)*
Plotkin Miss E. *(USA)*
Radwanska Miss A. *(Poland)*
Rakhim Miss A. *(Kazakhstan)*
Rebersak Miss P. *(Slovenia)*
Ripoll Miss D. *(Germany)*
Rodina Miss E. *(Russia)*
Savchuk Miss O. *(Ukraine)*
Schoofs Miss B. *(Netherlands)*
Sema Miss E. *(Japan)*
Shvedova Miss Y. *(Russia)*
Sweeting Miss J. *(Bahamas)*
Szatmari Miss A. *(Romania)*
Szavay Miss A. *(Hungary)*
Tatishvili Miss A. *(Georgia)*
Tetreault Miss V. *(Canada)*
Wozniacki Miss C. *(Denmark)*
Wozniak Miss A. *(Canada)*

BOYS

Arnaboldi A. *(Italy)*
Ball C. *(Australia)*
Bester P. *(Canada)*
Blake M. *(Great Britain)*
Bubka S. *(Ukraine)*
Carvalho R. *(Brazil)*
Chardy J. *(France)*
Chekhov P. *(Russia)*
Cilic M. *(Croatia)*
Coelho A. *(Australia)*
Damico K. *(USA)*
De Bakker T. *(Netherlands)*
Desein N. *(Belgium)*
Dolgopolov A. *(Ukraine)*
Farron-Mahon T. *(Ireland)*
Grangeiro L-H. *(Brazil)*
Haase R. *(Netherlands)*
Haider-Maurer A. *(Austria)*
Hunt J. *(USA)*
Jelenic P. *(Croatia)*
Kennaugh A. *(Great Britain)*
Khatib F. *(Great Britain)*
Kim S-Y. *(South Korea)*
Kirillov E. *(Russia)*
Levine J. *(USA)*
Lojda D. *(Czech Republic)*
Luisi P. *(Venezuela)*
Magdas A. *(Kuwait)*
Mayer L. *(Argentina)*
Miele A. *(Brazil)*
Murray A. *(Great Britain)*
Navarrete D. *(Venezuela)*
Nedunchezhiya J. *(India)*
Neilly T. *(USA)*
Querrey S. *(USA)*
Roshardt R. *(Switzerland)*
Sadecky A. *(Switzerland)*
Sayer M. *(Hong Kong)*
Schottler J. *(Germany)*
Shabaz M. *(USA)*
Shokeen V. *(India)*
Sijsling I. *(Netherlands)*
Singh S. *(India)*
Smyczek T. *(USA)*
Sweeting R. *(Bahamas)*
Tarasevitch S. *(Belarussia)*
Thron A. *(Germany)*
Van Der Duim A. *(Netherlands)*
Young D. *(USA)*

Bold figures denote position in singles draw.

EVENT I: THE GENTLEMEN'S SINGLES CHAMPIONSHIP 2005

HOLDER: R. FEDERER

The winner became the holder, for the year only, of the Challenge Cup and was presented by The All England Lawn Tennis and Croquet Club in 1887. The winner received a silver replica of the Challenge Cup. A silver salver was presented to the runner-up and a bronze medal to each defeated semi-finalist. The matches were the best of five sets.

First Round	Second Round	Third Round	Fourth Round	Quarter-Finals	Semi-Finals	Final

1. Federer, Roger [1] *(1)* (SUI)
2. Mathieu, Paul-Henri *(60)* (FRA)
3. Minar, Ivo *(96)* (CZE)
4. Tabara, Michal *(110)* (CZE)
(WC) 5. Goodall, Joshua *(318)* (GBR)
6. Di Mauro, Alessio *(92)* (ITA)
7. Benneteau, Julien *(129)* (FRA)
8. Kiefer, Nicolas [25] *(25)* (GER)
9. Ferrero, Juan Carlos [23] *(31)* (ESP)
(Q) 10. Delgado, Jamie *(213)* (GBR)
11. Enqvist, Thomas *(131)* (SWE)
12. Lee, Hyung-Taik *(68)* (KOR)
13. Mayer, Florian *(56)* (GER)
14. Ventura, Santiago *(111)* (ESP)
15. Verdasco, Fernando *(58)* (ESP)
16. Robredo, Tommy [13] *(13)* (ESP)
17. Johansson, Joachim [11] *(10)* (SWE)
18. Montanes, Albert *(80)* (ESP)
19. Martin, Alberto *(51)* (ESP)
20. Rusedski, Greg *(39)* (GBR)
21. Acasuso, Jose *(47)* (ARG)
22. Zib, Tomas *(61)* (CZE)
(WC) 23. Mackin, Alan *(221)* (GBR)
24. Gonzalez, Fernando [21] *(23)* (CHI)
25. Youzhny, Mikhail [31] *(34)* (RUS)
26. Baghdatis, Marcos *(88)* (CYP)
27. Hernandez, Oscar *(90)* (ESP)
28. Lisnard, Jean-Rene *(93)* (FRA)
29. Bjorkman, Jonas *(112)* (SWE)
(Q) 30. Morrison, Jeff *(107)* (USA)
31. Draper, Scott *(102)* (AUS)
32. Davydenko, Nikolay [8] *(7)* (RUS)
33. Hewitt, Lleyton [3] *(2)* (AUS)
34. Rochus, Christophe *(48)* (BEL)
35. Hernych, Jan *(77)* (CZE)
(WC) 36. Blake, James *(104)* (USA)
(LL) 37. Gimelstob, Justin *(124)* (USA)
(Q) 38. Garcia, Adrian *(170)* (CHI)
39. Sargsian, Sargis *(91)* (ARM)
40. Massu, Nicolas [29] *(29)* (CHI)
41. Dent, Taylor [24] *(30)* (USA)
(Q) 42. Norman, Dick *(104)* (BEL)
43. Kim, Kevin *(71)* (USA)
(WC) 44. Bogdanovic, Alex *(184)* (GBR)
(Q) 45. Dupuis, Anthony *(117)* (FRA)
46. Berdych, Tomas *(43)* (CZE)
47. Burgsmuller, Lars *(101)* (GER)
48. Puerta, Mariano [16] *(11)* (ARG)
49. Ancic, Mario [10] *(21)* (CRO)
(Q) 50. Summerer, Tobias *(179)* (GER)
(Q) 51. Udomchoke, Danai *(161)* (THA)
52. Koubek, Stefan *(78)* (AUT)
53. Monfils, Gael *(82)* (FRA)
(Q) 54. Okun, Noam *(152)* (ISR)
55. Saulnier, Cyril *(49)* (FRA)
56. Hrbaty, Dominik [22] *(24)* (SVK)
57. Lopez, Feliciano [26] *(33)* (ESP)
58. Phau, Bjorn *(103)* (GER)
(WC) 59. Sherwood, David *(260)* (GBR)
60. Mello, Ricardo *(54)* (BRA)
61. Beck, Karol *(45)* (SVK)
(WC) 62. Philippoussis, Mark *(188)* (AUS)
63. Srichaphan, Paradorn *(37)* (THA)
64. Safin, Marat [5] *(5)* (RUS)
65. Rochus, Olivier [33] *(36)* (BEL)
(LL) 66. Goldstein, Paul *(100)* (USA)
67. Mirnyi, Max *(40)* (BLR)
68. Schuettler, Rainer *(72)* (GER)
69. Wawrinka, Stanislas *(73)* (SUI)
70. Santoro, Fabrice *(53)* (FRA)
71. Wessels, Peter *(79)* (NED)
72. Novak, Jiri [28] *(28)* (CZE)
73. Haas, Tommy [19] *(22)* (GER)
74. Tipsarevic, Janko *(109)* (SCG)
(Q) 75. Lu, Yen-Hsun *(151)* (TPE)
(Q) 76. Clement, Arnaud *(105)* (FRA)
77. Pavel, Andrei *(42)* (ROM)
(Q) 78. Karanusic, Roko *(180)* (CRO)
79. Ulihrach, Bohdan *(119)* (CZE)
80. Johansson, Thomas [12] *(18)* (SWE)
81. Stepanek, Radek [14] *(15)* (CZE)
82. Ginepri, Robby *(74)* (USA)
(WC) 83. Murray, Andrew *(317)* (GBR)
(Q) 84. Bastl, George *(141)* (SUI)
85. Kucera, Karol *(101)* (SVK)
86. Horna, Luis *(55)* (PER)
87. Sluiter, Raemon *(99)* (NED)
88. Nalbandian, David [18] *(19)* (ARG)
89. Gasquet, Richard [27] *(27)* (FRA)
90. Kohlschreiber, Philipp *(64)* (GER)
(Q) 91. Elseneer, Gilles *(192)* (BEL)
92. Starace, Potito *(85)* (ITA)
93. Mantilla, Felix *(75)* (ESP)
94. Muller, Gilles *(69)* (LUX)
95. Spadea, Vincent *(41)* (USA)
96. Nadal, Rafael [4] *(3)* (ESP)
97. Henman, Tim [6] *(9)* (GBR)
98. Nieminen, Jarkko *(70)* (FIN)
99. Almagro, Nicolas *(76)* (ESP)
100. Tursunov, Dmitry *(76)* (RUS)
101. Popp, Alexander *(91)* (GER)
102. Haehnel, Jerome *(106)* (FRA)
103. Arthurs, Wayne *(86)* (AUS)
104. Volandri, Filippo [32] *(32)* (ITA)
105. Ferrer, David [17] *(16)* (ESP)
106. Garcia-Lopez, Guillermo *(81)* (ESP)
107. Monaco, Juan *(92)* (ARG)
(Q) 108. Djokovic, Novak *(127)* (SCG)
109. Hanescu, Victor *(57)* (ROM)
110. Carlsen, Kenneth *(52)* (DEN)
111. Llodra, Michael *(65)* (FRA)
112. Grosjean, Sebastien [9] *(26)* (FRA)
113. Coria, Guillermo [15] *(14)* (ARG)
114. Behrend, Tomas *(83)* (GER)
(WC) 115. Marray, Jonathan *(274)* (GBR)
116. Malisse, Xavier *(50)* (BEL)
117. Calatrava, Alex *(121)* (ESP)
(Q) 118. Ketola, Tuomas *(225)* (FIN)
119. Melzer, Jurgen *(38)* (AUT)
120. Ljubicic, Ivan [20] *(17)* (CRO)
121. Soderling, Robin [30] *(35)* (SWE)
122. Andreev, Igor *(44)* (RUS)
123. Sanguinetti, Davide *(63)* (ITA)
(Q) 124. Seppi, Andreas *(87)* (ITA)
(LL) 125. Bracciali, Daniele *(120)* (ITA)
126. Karlovic, Ivo *(59)* (CRO)
127. Vanek, Jiri *(97)* (CZE)
128. Roddick, Andy [2] *(4)* (USA)

Second Round

- R.Federer [1] 6/4 6/2 6/4
- I.Minar 6/4 6/4 6/4
- A.Di Mauro 6/3 7/6(4) 6/3
- N.Kiefer [25] 6/3 7/6(5) 5/7 3/6 6/4
- J.C.Ferrero [23] 7/6(2) 6/1 6/4
- H-T.Lee 6/3 6/7(4) 7/5 6/4
- F.Mayer 6/4 7/5 6/2
- F.Verdasco 6/1 6/2 7/5
- J.Johansson [11] 6/4 6/1 7/5
- G.Rusedski 6/3 4/6 6/2 6/1
- T.Zib 7/5 6/3 6/3
- F.Gonzalez [21] 6/3 6/4 6/4
- M.Youzhny [31] 6/2 3/6 6/1 6/4
- J-R.Lisnard 6/4 2/1 Ret'd
- J.Bjorkman 6/3 6/3 4/6 2/6 6/2
- N.Davydenko [8] 7/6(4) 6/4 6/3
- L.Hewitt [3] 6/3 6/3 6/1
- J.Hernych 1/6 6/4 7/6(6) 7/6(4)
- J.Gimelstob 6/4 6/2 6/1
- N.Massu [29] 7/6(7) 6/3 6/4
- T.Dent [24] 7/6(4) 7/6(4) 4/6 6/7(7) 6/2
- K.Kim 6/7(4) 6/1 6/4 6/2
- T.Berdych 7/6(5) 7/5 3/6 7/6(4)
- L.Burgsmuller 6/1 6/1 6/4
- M.Ancic [10] 6/3 7/5 6/1
- D.Udomchoke 5/7 6/4 4/6 6/3 8/6
- G.Monfils 3/6 6/4 6/4 7/6(14)
- D.Hrbaty [22] 7/6(0) 6/0 6/2
- F.Lopez [26] 5/7 7/6(8) 6/7(5) 6/2 6/4
- D.Sherwood 6/3 6/4 6/4
- M.Philippoussis 7/5 6/4 6/2
- M.Safin [5] 6/2 6/4 6/4
- O.Rochus [33] 6/4 6/2 6/2
- M.Mirnyi 6/3 6/3 6/4
- F.Santoro 6/2 6/7(7) 7/5 6/1
- J.Novak [28] 7/6(4) 6/3 6/4
- J.Tipsarevic 6/2 2/1 Ret'd
- Y.Lu 7/6(4) 0/6 1/3 6/3
- A.Pavel 6/2 4/6 6/2 6/4
- T.Johansson [12] 6/3 6/2 6/2
- R.Stepanek [14] 6/7(5) 6/3 6/4 6/2
- A.Murray 6/4 6/2 6/2
- K.Kucera 4/6 6/3 6/3 6/4
- D.Nalbandian [18] 6/2 6/2 7/5
- R.Gasquet [27] 6/3 3/6 6/3 6/2
- G.Elseneer 6/3 7/6(9) 6/3
- G.Muller 5/4 Ret'd
- R.Nadal [4] 6/4 6/3 6/0
- T.Henman [6] 3/6 6/7(5) 6/4 7/5 6/2
- D.Tursunov 7/6(2) 7/6(4) 6/3
- A.Popp 6/2 6/2 2/6 6/4
- W.Arthurs 6/3 6/4 6/4
- G.Garcia-Lopez 6/3 6/2 7/6(7)
- N.Djokovic 6/3 7/6(5) 6/3
- V.Hanescu 6/7(2) 7/6(4) 6/3 5/7 6/4
- S.Grosjean 3/6 7/5 4/6 7/6(5) 6/4
- G.Coria [15] 6/1 6/2 6/2
- X.Malisse 6/3 3/6 2/6 6/1 6/4
- A.Calatrava 4/6 7/6(4) 6/3 6/1
- J.Melzer 6/4 6/4 6/4
- I.Andreev 6/7(3) 7/5 6/3 6/3
- D.Sanguinetti 6/3 6/2 6/1
- D.Bracciali 6/7(4) 7/6(8) 3/6 6/2 12/10
- A.Roddick [2] 6/1 7/6(4) 6/2

Third Round

- R.Federer [1] 6/4 6/4 6/1
- N.Kiefer [25] 6/3 7/5 6/3
- J.C.Ferrero [23] 6/4 3/6 4/6 6/3 6/3
- F.Mayer 7/6(6) 7/6 6/3
- J.Johansson [11] 7/6(10) 3/6 6/4 7/6(5)
- F.Gonzalez [21] 6/4 7/6(6) 6/3
- M.Youzhny [31] 1/6 7/5 6/3 6/4
- J.Bjorkman 6/7(4) 1/2 Ret'd
- L.Hewitt [3] 6/2 7/5 3/6 6/3
- J.Gimelstob 6/3 4/6 7/6(5) 7/6(0)
- T.Dent [24] 6/3 6/4 6/4
- T.Berdych 6/3 6/3 6/1
- M.Ancic [10] 7/6(6) 3/6 6/3 6/3
- G.Monfils 6/3 6/1 6/4 7/5
- F.Lopez [26] 6/2 6/4 6/2
- M.Safin [5] 7/6(4) 7/6(4) 6/4
- M.Mirnyi 7/6(4) 6/2 7/6(3)
- J.Novak [28] 6/1 4/6 7/6(4) 6/3
- J.Tipsarevic 2/6 6/3 6/2 4/6 7/5
- T.Johansson [12] 3/6 7/6(4) 7/4(4) 6/1
- A.Murray 6/4 6/4 6/4
- D.Nalbandian [18] 6/2 6/4 6/3
- R.Gasquet [27] 7/6(7) 7/6(3) 6/7(3) 6/2
- G.Muller 6/4 4/6 6/3 6/4
- D.Tursunov 3/6 6/2 3/6 6/3 8/6
- A.Popp 6/3 6/7(4) 3/6 7/6(4) 14/12
- N.Djokovic 3/6 3/6 7/6(5) 7/6(3) 6/4
- S.Grosjean 6/3 6/4 6/2
- G.Coria [15] 3/6 6/3 7/5 6/7(3) 6/4
- J.Melzer 6/4 6/1 6/1
- I.Andreev 6/4 6/2 6/3
- A.Roddick [2] 7/5 6/3 6/7(3) 4/6 6/3

Fourth Round

- R.Federer [1] 6/2 6/7(5) 6/1 7/5
- J.C.Ferrero [23] 3/6 6/2 6/1 6/1
- F.Gonzalez [21] 6/4 6/4 6/2
- M.Youzhny [31] 7/5 6/3 3/6 7/6(9)
- L.Hewitt [3] 7/6(5) 6/4 7/5
- T.Dent [24] 6/3 7/6(5) 6/3
- M.Ancic [10] 6/3 6/3 6/1
- F.Lopez [26] 6/2 6/4 6/3
- M.Mirnyi 5/7 7/5 6/4 7/6(2)
- T.Johansson [12] 6/2 6/3 6/1
- D.Nalbandian [18] 6/7(4) 1/6 6/0 6/4 6/1
- R.Gasquet [27] 7/6(3) 6/3 6/3
- D.Tursunov 5/7 7/6(5) 6/2 6/2
- S.Grosjean 7/5 6/4 5/7 6/4
- G.Coria [15] 3/6 3/6 6/2 6/2 6/4
- A.Roddick [2] 6/2 6/2 7/6(4)

Quarter-Finals

- R.Federer [1] 6/3 6/4 7/6(6)
- F.Gonzalez [21] 7/6(3) 7/6(5) 6/3
- L.Hewitt [3] 6/4 6/4 6/7(7) 6/3
- F.Lopez [26] 6/4 6/4 6/2
- T.Johansson [12] 6/4 7/5 6/4
- D.Nalbandian [18] 6/4 7/6(3) 6/0
- S.Grosjean [9] 6/4 6/7(5) 6/3 3/6 6/1
- A.Roddick [2] 6/3 7/6(1) 6/4

Semi-Finals

- R.Federer [1] 7/5 6/2 7/6(2)
- L.Hewitt [3] 7/5 6/4 7/6(2)
- T.Johansson [12] 7/6(5) 6/2 6/2
- A.Roddick [2] 6/7(6) 6/2 6/2 6/7(10) 7/6(5)

Final

- R.Federer [1] 6/2 7/6(2) 6/4

EVENT II: THE GENTLEMEN'S DOUBLES CHAMPIONSHIP 2005
HOLDERS: J. BJORKMAN & T.A. WOODBRIDGE

The winners became the holders, for the year only, of the Challenge Cups presented by the Oxford University Lawn Tennis Club in 1884 and the late Sir Herbert Wilberforce in 1937. The winners received a silver replica of the Challenge Cup. A silver salver was presented to each of the runners-up, and a bronze medal to each defeated semi-finalist. The matches were the best of five sets.

First Round	Second Round	Third Round	Quarter-Finals	Semi-Finals	Final
1. J.Bjorkman (SWE) & M.Mirnyi (BLR) [1]	J.Bjorkman & M.Mirnyi [1] 6/0 6/3 5/7 4/6 6/4	J.Bjorkman & M.Mirnyi [1] 6/7(1) 4/6 6/3 6/4 6/3			
(WC) 2. R.Barker (GBR) & W.Barker (GBR)					
3. J.Kerr (AUS) & J.Thomas (USA)	A.Fisher & C.Haggard 6/4 6/4 7/6(6)				
4. A.Fisher (AUS) & C.Haggard (RSA)					
5. I.Ljubicic (CRO) & U.Vico (ITA)	V.Hanescu & A.Pavel 6/3 6/4 6/4	J.Knowle & J.Melzer [13] 7/6(2) 7/6(5) 7/5			
6. V.Hanescu (ROM) & A.Pavel (ROM)					
7. J.Acasuso (ARG) & A.Martin (ESP)	J.Knowle & J.Melzer [13] 6/3 6/2 6/3			J.Bjorkman & M.Mirnyi [1] 7/5 6/3 6/2	
8. J.Knowle (AUT) & J.Melzer (AUT) [13]					
9. C.Suk (CZE) & P.Vizner (CZE) [11]	C.Suk & P.Vizner [11] 6/3 6/7(8) 7/6(6) 7/6(3)	C.Suk & P.Vizner [11] 6/4 5/7 7/6(8) 1/6 7/5	R.Schuettler & A.Waske 6/4 6/4 7/6(6)		
10. J.Gimelstob (USA) & B.MacPhie (USA)					
11. M.Fyrstenberg (POL) & M.Matkowski (POL)	M.Fyrstenberg & M.Matkowski 6/3 6/2 6/4				
12. J.Monaco (ARG) & F.Verdasco (ESP)					
13. J.Hernych (CZE) & T.Zib (CZE)	J.Hernych & T.Zib o/6 7/6(4) 7/6(7) 4/6 6/3	R.Schuettler & A.Waske 6/4 6/7(1) 6/7(2) 6/2 7/5			
14. J.Novak (CZE) & P.Pala (CZE)					
15. R.Schuettler (GER) & A.Waske (GER)	R.Schuettler & A.Waske 5/7 5/7 7/6(5) 7/5 7/5				S.Huss & W.Moodie 2/6 6/2 6/4 7/6(4)
16. W.Arthurs (AUS) & P.Hanley (AUS) [7]					
17. M.Knowles (BAH) & M.Llodra (FRA) [3]	M.Knowles & M.Llodra [3] 6/2 6/4 6/3	M.Knowles & M.Llodra [3] 6/4 7/6(1) 6/4			
18. R.Koenig (RSA) & S.Prieto (ARG)					
19. G.Galimberti (ITA) & D.Sanguinetti (ITA)	R.Lindstedt & A.Peya 7/6(3) 6/2 6/3				
(Q) 20. R.Lindstedt (SWE) & A.Peya (AUT)					
(WC) 21. M.Hilton (GBR) & J.Marray (GBR)	M.Hilton & J.Marray 6/7(3) 6/4 7/6(3) 7/5	I.Karlovic & R.Wassen 4/6 6/3 2/6 6/1 7/5	M.Knowles & M.Llodra [3] 6/4 6/4 5/7 6/4		
22. J.Benneteau (FRA) & N.Mahut (FRA)					
23. I.Karlovic (CRO) & R.Wassen (NED)	I.Karlovic & R.Wassen 7/5 6/3 6/4				
24. Y.Allegro (SUI) & M.Kohlmann (GER) [16]					
25. F.Cermak (CZE) & L.Friedl (CZE) [9]	F.Cermak & L.Friedl [9] 7/6(4) 6/3 6/1	F.Cermak & L.Friedl [9] 3/6 6/3 7/6(2) 6/3		S.Huss & W.Moodie 6/4 6/4 6/4	
(Q) 26. R.Delgado (PAR) & A.Sa (BRA)					
(WC) 27. A.Banks (GBR) & A.R.Mackin (GBR)	T.Ketola & F.Niemeyer 7/5 7/6(2) 6/3				
(Q) 28. T.Ketola (FIN) & F.Niemeyer (CAN)					
29. C.Saulnier (FRA) & T.Vanhoudt (BEL)	S.Huss & W.Moodie 6/7(5) 6/3 6/2 6/3	S.Huss & W.Moodie 6/3 7/6(3) 6/3	S.Huss & W.Moodie 6/2 6/3 6/4		
(Q) 30. S.Huss (AUS) & W.Moodie (RSA)					
31. G.Oliver (USA) & J.Palmer (USA)	M.Bhupathi & T.A.Woodbridge [6] 6/4 6/2 6/7(5) 6/3				
32. M.Bhupathi (IND) & T.A.Woodbridge (AUS) [6]					
33. L.Paes (IND) & N.Zimonjic (SCG) [5]	L.Paes & N.Zimonjic [5] 7/6(3) 6/7(5) 6/3	L.Paes & N.Zimonjic [5] 3/6 6/3 6/4 7/6(3)			S.Huss & W.Moodie 7/6(4) 6/3 6/7(2) 6/3
34. L.Arnold (ARG) & D.Bracciali (ITA)					
35. J.Coetzee (RSA) & R.Mello (BRA)	R.Leach & T.Parrott 6/3 6/1 6/7(3) 3/6 6/2				
36. R.Leach (USA) & T.Parrott (USA)					
37. M.Garcia (ARG) & L.Horna (PER)	K.Beck & J.Levinsky 6/3 6/2 3/6 6/3	K.Beck & J.Levinsky 7/6(3) 6/7(2) 2/6 6/4 6/4	L.Paes & N.Zimonjic [5] 7/5 6/3 6/4		
38. K.Beck (SVK) & J.Levinsky (CZE)					
(WC) 39. A.Murray (GBR) & D.Sherwood (GBR)	M.Damm & M.Hood [10] 6/1 6/4 6/4				
40. M.Damm (CZE) & M.Hood (ARG) [10]					
41. G.Etlis (ARG) & M.Rodriguez (ARG) [14]	G.Etlis & M.Rodriguez [14] 6/2 6/1 7/6(2)	G.Etlis & M.Rodriguez [14] 3/6 6/4 Ret'd		W.Black & K.Ullyett [4] 7/5 7/6(8) 7/6(8)	
42. E.Artoni (ITA) & M.Puerta (ARG)					
(LL) 43. R.Hutchins (GBR) & M.Lee (GBR)	J-F.Bachelot & A.Clement 6/3 7/6(2) 6/2				
44. J-F.Bachelot (FRA) & A.Clement (FRA)					
(WC) 45. A.Bogdanovic (GBR) & J.Goodall (GBR)	T.Berdych & F.Mayer 6/2 6/4 6/4	W.Black & K.Ullyett [4] 6/4 6/1 6/2	W.Black & K.Ullyett [4] 6/4 6/2 3/6 7/6(3)		
46. T.Berdych (CZE) & F.Mayer (GER)					
47. M.Bertolini (ITA) & F.Volandri (ITA)	W.Black & K.Ullyett [4] 6/1 6/2 6/2				
48. W.Black (ZIM) & K.Ullyett (ZIM) [4]					B.Bryan & M.Bryan [2] 4/6 6/3 6/4 6/4
49. S.Aspelin (SWE) & T.Perry (AUS) [8]	D.Hrbaty & M.Mertinak 2/6 6/7(2) 7/6(5) 6/3 6/3	D.Hrbaty & M.Mertinak walk over			
50. D.Hrbaty (SVK) & M.Mertinak (SVK)					
51. F.Lopez (ESP) & R.Nadal (ESP)	F.Lopez & R.Nadal 6/3 7/6(3) 7/6(9)				
52. T.Cibulec (CZE) & D.Rikl (CZE)				D.Hrbaty & M.Mertinak 6/1 6/3 6/3	
53. G.Muller (LUX) & C.Rochus (BEL)	X.Malisse & O.Rochus 6/4 7/5 3/6 3/6 6/2	X.Malisse & O.Rochus 6/1 7/6(7) 6/2			
54. X.Malisse (BEL) & O.Rochus (BEL)					
(LL) 55. L.Dlouhy (CZE) & D.Skoch (CZE)	F.Gonzalez & N.Massu [12] 3/6 6/4 7/6(5) 6/3				
56. F.Gonzalez (CHI) & N.Massu (CHI) [12]				B.Bryan & M.Bryan [2] 7/6(2) 6/4 7/6(1)	
57. J.Erlich (ISR) & A.Ram (ISR) [15]	J.Erlich & A.Ram [15] 6/4 6/7(5) 6/4 6/2	J.Erlich & A.Ram [15] walk over			
(WC) 58. J.Delgado (GBR) & A.Parmar (GBR)					
59. J.Landsberg (SWE) & R.Soderling (SWE)	J.Landsberg & R.Soderling 6/3 6/2 6/4				
60. A.Lopez Moron (ESP) & T.Robredo (ESP)					
61. K.Kim (USA) & H-T.Lee (KOR)	J.Auckland & D.Kiernan 6/7(3) 1/6 6/4 6/3 6/4	B.Bryan & M.Bryan [2] 6/3 7/6(0) 6/3	B.Bryan & M.Bryan [2] 6/3 7/6(0) 6/3		
(WC) 62. J.Auckland (GBR) & D.Kiernan (GBR)					
63. D.Ferrer (ESP) & S.Ventura (ESP)	B.Bryan & M.Bryan [2] 5/7 6/3 6/2 6/0				
64. B.Bryan (USA) & M.Bryan (USA) [2]					

Heavy type denotes seeded players. The figure in brackets against names denotes the order in which they were seeded.
(WC)=Wild card. (Q)=Qualifier. (LL)=Lucky loser.

EVENT III: THE LADIES' SINGLES CHAMPIONSHIP 2005

HOLDER: MISS M. SHARAPOVA

The winner became the holder, for the year only, of the Challenge Trophy presented by The All England Lawn Tennis and Croquet Club in 1886. The winner received a silver replica of the Trophy. A silver salver was presented to the runner-up and a bronze medal to each defeated semi-finalist. The matches were the best of three sets.

First Round

1. **Davenport, Lindsay [1]** (1) (USA)
2. Jidkova, Alina (78) (RUS)
3. Marrero, Marta (126) (ESP)
(Q) 4. Jackson, Jamea (108) (USA)
5. Strycova, Barbora (114) (CZE)
6. Osterloh, Lilia (101) (USA)
7. Mamic, Sanda (86) (CRO)
8. **Safina, Dinara [30]** (33) (RUS)
9. **Sugiyama, Ai [23]** (25) (JPN)
10. Vinci, Roberta (111) (ITA)
11. Spears, Abigail (69) (USA)
12. Kremer, Anne (106) (LUX)
13. Irvin, Marissa (91) (USA)
(Q) 14. Obata, Saori (151) (JPN)
(WC) 15. O'Brien, Katie (322) (GBR)
16. **Clijsters, Kim [15]** (17) (BEL)
17. **Schnyder, Patty [10]** (11) (SUI)
18. Serra Zanetti, Antonella (82) (ITA)
19. Perebiynis, Tatiana (119) (UKR)
(Q) 20. Arvidsson, Sofia (140) (SWE)
21. Kirilenko, Maria (53) (RUS)
(Q) 22. Callens, Els (165) (BEL)
23. Maleeva, Magdalena (38) (BUL)
24. **Asagoe, Shinobu [24]** (26) (JPN)
25. **Vaidisova, Nicole [27]** (30) (CZE)
26. Kostanic, Jelena (60) (CRO)
27. Stosur, Samantha (49) (AUS)
28. Pastikova, Michaela (104) (CZE)
29. Morigami, Akiko (64) (JPN)
30. Mirza, Sania (72) (IND)
(WC) 31. Llewellyn, Rebecca (437) (GBR)
32. **Kuznetsova, Svetlana [5]** (5) (RUS)
33. **Mauresmo, Amelie [3]** (3) (FRA)
(LL) 34. Czink, Melinda (133) (HUN)
35. Sanchez Lorenzo, Maria (88) (ESP)
36. Domachowska, Marta (48) (POL)
(WC) 37. Borwell, Sarah (317) (GBR)
38. Perry, Shenay (150) (USA)
39. Tanasugarn, Tamarine (66) (THA)
40. **Sprem, Karolina [25]** (28) (CRO)
41. **Farina Elia, Silvia [22]** (24) (ITA)
42. Sucha, Martina (79) (SVK)
43. Vento-Kabchi, Maria (55) (VEN)
44. Sequera, Milagros (116) (VEN)
45. Shaughnessy, Meghann (70) (USA)
46. Schruff, Julia (90) (GER)
47. Smashnova, Anna (57) (ISR)
48. **Likhovtseva, Elena [13]** (15) (RUS)
49. **Myskina, Anastasia [9]** (10) (RUS)
(Q) 50. Bohmova, Katerina (147) (CZE)
51. Dominikovic, Evie (102) (AUS)
52. Nakamura, Aiko (92) (JPN)
53. Diaz-Oliva, Mariana (76) (ARG)
(WC) 54. Keothavong, Anne (264) (GBR)
55. Chakvetadze, Anna (43) (RUS)
56. **Jankovic, Jelena [17]** (19) (SCG)
57. **Frazier, Amy [28]** (31) (USA)
58. Washington, Mashona (59) (USA)
59. Sfar, Selima (110) (TUN)
(WC) 60. Loit, Emilie (96) (FRA)
(Q) 61. Baltacha, Elena (120) (GBR)
62. Klaschka, Sabine (179) (GER)
63. Benesova, Iveta (52) (CZE)
64. **Dementieva, Elena [6]** (6) (RUS)
65. **Henin-Hardenne, Justine [7]** (7) (BEL)
66. Daniilidou, Eleni (73) (GRE)
67. Koukalova, Klara (41) (CZE)
68. Granville, Laura (63) (USA)
69. Dulko, Gisela (37) (ARG)
70. Fedak, Yuliana (94) (UKR)
71. Gagliardi, Emmanuelle (74) (SUI)
72. **Pennetta, Flavia [26]** (29) (ITA)
73. **Ivanovic, Ana [19]** (21) (SCG)
74. Douchevina, Vera (54) (RUS)
75. Chladkova, Denisa (71) (CZE)
76. Foretz, Stephanie (117) (FRA)
(Q) 77. Vakulenko, Julia (223) (UKR)
78. Garbin, Tathiana (95) (ITA)
79. Safarova, Lucie (80) (CZE)
80. **Pierce, Mary [12]** (13) (FRA)
81. **Williams, Venus [14]** (16) (USA)
82. Birnerova, Eva (112) (CZE)
83. Pratt, Nicole (124) (AUS)
84. Cervanova, Ludmila (85) (SVK)
(Q) 85. Tu, Meilen (153) (USA)
86. Peer, Shahar (62) (ISR)
87. Linetskaya, Evgenia (39) (RUS)
88. **Hantuchova, Daniela [20]** (22) (SVK)
89. **Bartoli, Marion [29]** (32) (FRA)
90. Fujiwara, Rika (97) (JPN)
(Q) 91. Harkleroad, Ashley (204) (USA)
92. Craybas, Jill (83) (USA)
93. Santangelo, Mara (127) (ITA)
(Q) 94. Poutchek, Tatiana (218) (BLR)
95. Haynes, Angela (103) (USA)
96. **Williams, Serena [4]** (4) (USA)
97. **Petrova, Nadia [8]** (8) (RUS)
98. Ruano Pascual, Virginia (87) (ESP)
99. Schaul, Claudine (162) (LUX)
(LL) 100. Beltrame, Severine (118) (FRA)
101. Ondraskova, Zuzana (75) (CZE)
(WC) 102. Black, Cara (172) (ZIM)
103. Castano, Catalina (77) (COL)
104. **Razzano, Virginie [32]** (35) (FRA)
105. **Schiavone, Francesca [21]** (23) (ITA)
106. Brandi, Kristina (67) (PUR)
107. Martinez, Conchita (47) (ESP)
(Q) 108. Bondarenko, Katerina (234) (UKR)
109. Peschke, Kveta (61) (CZE)
110. Randriantefy, Dally (46) (MAD)
111. Weingartner, Marlene (154) (GER)
112. **Zvonareva, Vera [11]** (18) (RUS)
113. **Dechy, Nathalie [16]** (18) (FRA)
114. Camerin, Maria Elena (68) (ITA)
(WC) 115. O'Donoghue, Jane (232) (GBR)
116. Groenefeld, Anna-Lena (40) (GER)
117. Panova, Tatiana (93) (RUS)
118. Raymond, Lisa (50) (USA)
119. Bondarenko, Alyona (89) (UKR)
120. **Golovin, Tatiana [18]** (20) (FRA)
121. **Medina Garrigues, Anabel [31]** (34) (ESP)
122. Srebotnik, Katarina (58) (SLO)
123. Cho, Yoon Jeong (84) (KOR)
124. Parra Santonja, Arantxa (81) (ESP)
(WC) 125. Janes, Amanda (222) (GBR)
126. Karatantcheva, Sesil (51) (BUL)
127. Llagostera Vives, Nuria (36) (ESP)
128. **Sharapova, Maria [2]** (2) (RUS)

Second Round

- Miss L.Davenport [1] 6/0 6/2
- Miss J.Jackson 6/2 6/3
- Miss B.Strycova 6/3 7/5
- Miss D.Safina [30] 6/3 6/4
- Miss R.Vinci 6/2 2/6 6/4
- Miss A.Kremer 6/2 6/2
- Miss M.Irvin 7/6(4) 6/3
- Miss K.Clijsters [15] 6/2 6/3
- Miss A.Serra Zanetti 6/4 6/7(7) 6/3
- Miss S.Arvidsson 6/3 7/6(5)
- Miss M.Kirilenko 6/2 7/6(3)
- Miss M.Maleeva 6/2 7/6(6)
- Miss N.Vaidisova [27] 6/3 3/6 6/3
- Miss M.Pastikova 7/6(1) 6/4
- Miss S.Mirza 6/3 3/6 8/6
- Miss S.Kuznetsova [5] 6/0 6/1
- Miss A.Mauresmo [3] 6/4 6/2
- Miss M.Sanchez Lorenzo 6/4 4/6 6/2
- Miss S.Perry 7/6(11) 6/3
- Miss T.Tanasugarn 6/2 6/2
- Mrs S.Farina Elia 6/4 6/2
- Mrs M.Vento-Kabchi 7/6(1) 4/6 6/4
- Miss M.Shaughnessy 6/1 1/6 6/2
- Miss E.Likhovtseva [13] 6/2 6/2
- Miss A.Myskina [9] 5/7 7/6(4) 6/4
- Miss A.Nakamura 5/7 6/3 6/4
- Miss M.Diaz-Oliva 6/3 6/4
- Miss J.Jankovic [17] 6/4 6/2
- Miss M.Washington 6/4 4/6 6/4
- Miss S.Sfar 6/2 4/6 9/7
- Miss S.Klaschka 6/3 6/2
- Miss E.Dementieva [6] 6/2 6/3
- Miss E.Daniilidou 7/6(8) 2/6 7/5
- Miss L.Granville 6/1 6/2
- Miss G.Dulko 6/2 6/4
- Miss F.Pennetta [26] 6/1 6/2
- Miss A.Ivanovic 6/4 6/3
- Miss S.Foretz 6/3 4/6 6/1
- Miss J.Vakulenko 6/2 6/4
- Miss M.Pierce [12] 6/3 6/4
- Miss V.Williams [14] 6/2 6/4
- Miss N.J.Pratt 3/6 6/3 6/1
- Miss S.Peer 6/3 6/3
- Miss D.Hantuchova [20] 3/6 6/2 6/2
- Miss M.Bartoli [29] 6/2 6/2
- Miss J.Craybas 6/4 4/6 6/4
- Miss M.Santangelo 6/3 6/2
- Miss S.Williams [4] 6/7(12) 6/4 6/2
- Miss N.Petrova [8] 4/6 6/3 6/2
- Miss S.Beltrame 6/2 6/1
- Miss C.Black 6/3 6/3
- Miss V.Razzano [32] 6/7(6) 6/3 6/4
- Miss K.Brandi 6/3 3/6 9/7
- Miss C.Martinez 6/1 7/6(4)
- Mrs K.Peschke 7/5 6/1
- Miss V.Zvonareva [11] 2/6 6/4 6/0
- Miss N.Dechy [16] 7/6(1) 6/1
- Miss J.O'Donoghue 1/6 6/1 6/4
- Miss T.Panova 7/5 6/3
- Miss A.Bondarenko 6/3 3/6 7/5
- Miss K.Srebotnik 6/3 6/3
- Miss Y.J.Cho 6/3 6/3
- Miss S.Karatantcheva 7/5 6/7(6) 7/5
- Miss M.Sharapova [2] 6/2 6/2

Third Round

- Miss L.Davenport [1] 6/0 6/3
- Miss D.Safina [30] 6/2 6/2
- Miss R.Vinci 6/3 6/2
- Miss K.Clijsters [15] 6/1 6/1
- Miss A.Serra Zanetti 7/5 2/6 7/5
- Miss M.Maleeva 6/2 6/3
- Miss N.Vaidisova [27] 7/5 6/3
- Miss S.Kuznetsova [5] 6/4 6/7(4) 6/4
- Miss A.Mauresmo [3] 6/1 6/3
- Miss S.Perry 7/6(1) 6/2
- Mrs S.Farina Elia [22] 6/1 5/7 6/3
- Miss E.Likhovtseva [13] 6/3 7/6(4)
- Miss A.Myskina [9] 6/4 6/3
- Miss J.Jankovic [17] 6/3 7/5
- Miss M.Washington 6/3 3/6 6/3
- Miss E.Dementieva [6] 2/6 6/3 8/6
- Miss E.Daniilidou 6/2 6/0
- Miss F.Pennetta [26] 6/2 6/4
- Miss A.Ivanovic [19] 6/4 6/3
- Miss M.Pierce [12] 4/6 7/6(7) 9/7
- Miss V.Williams [14] 7/5 6/3
- Miss D.Hantuchova [20] 6/2 2/6 6/3
- Miss J.Craybas 6/1 6/4
- Miss S.Williams [4] 2/6 6/3 6/2
- Miss N.Petrova [8] 6/1 6/2
- Miss C.Black 6/4 7/6(5)
- Miss C.Martinez 6/2 6/3
- Mrs K.Peschke 1/6 6/4 6/3
- Miss N.Dechy [16] 6/2 6/1
- Miss A.Bondarenko 6/3 2/6 6/3
- Miss K.Srebotnik 7/5 6/4
- Miss M.Sharapova [2] 6/0 6/1

Fourth Round

- Miss L.Davenport [1] 6/2 6/1
- Miss K.Clijsters [15] 6/3 6/4
- Miss M.Maleeva 6/3 6/2
- Miss S.Kuznetsova [5] 7/5 6/7(5) 6/2
- Miss A.Mauresmo [3] 6/0 6/2
- Miss E.Likhovtseva [13] 5/7 6/4 6/4
- Miss A.Myskina [9] 6/0 5/7 10/8
- Miss E.Dementieva [6] 7/5 6/1
- Miss F.Pennetta [26] 6/4 6/3
- Miss M.Pierce [12] 6/1 6/4
- Miss V.Williams [14] 7/5 6/3
- Miss J.Craybas 6/3 7/6(4)
- Miss N.Petrova [8] 6/4 6/3
- Mrs K.Peschke 4/6 6/1
- Miss N.Dechy [16] 6/1 6/4
- Miss M.Sharapova [2] 6/2 6/4

Quarter-Finals

- Miss L.Davenport [1] 6/3 6/7(4) 6/3
- Miss S.Kuznetsova [5] 6/4 6/3
- Miss A.Mauresmo [3] 6/4 6/0
- Miss A.Myskina [9] 1/6 7/6(9) 7/5
- Miss M.Pierce [12] 6/3 6/1
- Miss V.Williams [14] 6/0 6/2
- Miss N.Petrova [8] 6/7(5) 7/6(7) 6/3
- Miss M.Sharapova [2] 6/4 6/2

Semi-Finals

- Miss L.Davenport [1] 7/6(1) 6/3
- Miss A.Mauresmo [3] 6/3 6/4
- Miss V.Williams [14] 6/0 7/6(10)
- Miss M.Sharapova [2] 7/6(6) 6/3

Final

- Miss L.Davenport [1] 6/7(5) 7/6(4) 6/4
- Miss V.Williams [14] 7/6(2) 6/1

Winner

- Miss V.Williams [14] 4/6 7/6(4) 9/7

EVENT IV: THE LADIES' DOUBLES CHAMPIONSHIP 2005
HOLDERS: MISS C. BLACK & MISS R.P. STUBBS

The winners became the holders, for the year only, of the Challenge Cups presented by H.R.H. Princess Marina, Duchess of Kent, the late President of The All England Lawn Tennis and Croquet Club in 1949 and The All England Lawn Tennis and Croquet Club in 2001. The winners received a silver replica of the Challenge Cup. A silver salver was presented to each of the runners-up and a bronze medal to each defeated semi-finalist. The matches were the best of three sets.

First Round	Second Round	Third Round	Quarter-Finals	Semi-Finals	Final
1. **Miss E.S.H.Callens** (BEL) **& Miss E.Gagliardi** (SUI) **[17]**	**Miss E.S.H.Callens & Miss E.Gagliardi [17]** 6/3 7/6(4)	**Miss E.S.H.Callens & Miss E.Gagliardi [17]** 6/1 6/2			
2. Mrs S.Farina Elia (ITA) & Miss R.Vinci (ITA)			Miss V.Douchevina & Miss S.Peer 5/7 6/3 7/5		
3. Miss M.Diaz-Oliva (ARG) & Miss M.Sucha (SVK)	Miss E.Baltacha & Miss J.O'Donoghue 7/5 1/6 6/1				
(WC) 4. Miss E.Baltacha (GBR) & Miss J.O'Donoghue (GBR)					
5. Miss J.Craybas (USA) & Miss M.Weingartner (GER)	Miss V.Douchevina & Miss S.Peer 7/6(4) 7/6(9)	Miss V.Douchevina & Miss S.Peer 6/2 6/7(7) 8/6			
6. Miss V.Douchevina (RUS) & Miss S.Peer (ISR)				**Miss A-L.Groenefeld & Miss M.Navratilova [8]** 7/6(5) 6/4	
7. Miss N.Dechy (FRA) & Miss K.Sprem (CRO)	**Miss G.Navratilova & Miss M.Pastikova [16]** 7/6(6) 6/4				
8. **Miss G.Navratilova** (CZE) **& Miss M.Pastikova** (CZE) **[16]**					
9. Miss S.Asagoe (JPN) & Miss K.Srebotnik (SLO) **[10]**	**Miss S.Asagoe & Miss K.Srebotnik [10]** 6/0 3/6 6/3	**Miss S.Asagoe & Miss K.Srebotnik [10]** 3/6 6/2 6/3			
10. Miss M.Marrero (ESP) & Miss A.Parra Santonja (ESP)			Miss A-L.Groenefeld & Miss M.Navratilova [8] 6/3 6/3		
11. Miss A.Kremer (LUX) & Miss A.Smashnova (ISR)	Miss E.Dominikovic & Miss A.Nakamura 6/3 3/6 6/2				
(Q) 12. Miss E.Dominikovic (AUS) & Miss A.Nakamura (JPN)					
13. Miss D.Chladkova (CZE) & Miss V.Razzano (FRA)	Miss D.Chladkova & Miss V.Razzano 6/4 6/3	**Miss A-L.Groenefeld & Miss M.Navratilova [8]** 6/1 6/4			
14. Miss E.Linetskaya (RUS) & Miss N.Vaidisova (CZE)					
(Q) 15. Miss R.Fujiwara (JPN) & Miss S.Obata (JPN)	**Miss A-L.Groenefeld & Miss M.Navratilova [8]** 6/3 6/3				
16. **Miss A-L.Groenefeld** (GER) **& Miss M.Navratilova** (USA) **[8]**					Miss S.Kuznetsova & Miss A.Mauresmo 6/4 6/4
17. **Miss L.M.Raymond** (USA) **& Miss R.P.Stubbs** (AUS) **[3]**	Miss S.Cohen-Aloro & Miss S.Sfar 6/4 3/6 6/2				
18. Miss S.Cohen-Aloro (FRA) & Miss S.Sfar (TUN)			Miss L.McShea & Miss A.Spears 6/1 6/2		
19. Miss L.McShea (AUS) & Miss A.Spears (USA)	Miss L.McShea & Miss A.Spears 6/7(4) 6/1 6/1				
(Q) 20. Miss T.Poutchek (BLR) & Miss Y.Akimova (BLR)					
21. Miss S.Kuznetsova (RUS) & Miss A.Mauresmo (FRA)	Miss S.Kuznetsova & Miss A.Mauresmo 7/5 6/2	Miss S.Kuznetsova & Miss A.Mauresmo 6/1 6/2			
22. Miss L.Cervanova (SVK) & Miss K.Koukalova (CZE)			Miss S.Kuznetsova & Miss A.Mauresmo 7/6(3) 6/2		
23. Miss L.Granville (USA) & Miss J.Lee (TPE)	Miss L.Granville & Miss J.Lee 3/6 6/4 6/0				
24. **Miss G.Dulko** (ARG) **& Mrs M.Vento-Kabchi** (VEN) **[13]**				Miss S.Kuznetsova & Miss A.Mauresmo 6/3 6/7(4) 6/1	
25. **Miss L.Davenport** (USA) **& Miss C.Morariu** (USA) **[12]**	**Miss L.Davenport & Miss C.Morariu [12]** 7/5 6/3				
26. Miss J.Jankovic (SCG) & Miss J.Kostanic (CRO)		Miss M.Bartoli & Miss M.Sequera 7/6(2) 3/6 6/4			
27. Miss M.Camerin (ITA) & Miss T.Garbin (ITA)	Miss M.Bartoli & Miss M.Sequera 6/0 6/4				
28. Miss M.Bartoli (FRA) & Miss M.Sequera (VEN)			Miss E.Likhovtseva & Miss V.Zvonareva [5] 6/4 3/6 6/3		
29. Miss J.Hopkins (USA) & Miss M.Washington (USA)	Miss J.Hopkins & Miss M.Washington 7/6(5) 6/1	**Miss E.Likhovtseva & Miss V.Zvonareva [5]** 6/7(5) 6/2 6/1			
30. Miss I.Benesova (CZE) & Miss G.Voskoboeva (RUS)					
(Q) 31. Miss A.Bondarenko (UKR) & Miss A.Rodionova (RUS)	**Miss E.Likhovtseva & Miss V.Zvonareva [5]** 6/2 7/5				
32. **Miss E.Likhovtseva** (RUS) **& Miss V.Zvonareva** (RUS) **[5]**					
33. **Miss J.Husarova** (SVK) **& Miss C.Martinez** (ESP) **[6]**	**Miss J.Husarova & Miss C.Martinez [6]** 6/2 1/6 6/1	**Miss J.Husarova & Miss C.Martinez [6]** 6/2 6/3			
34. Miss E.Birnerova (CZE) & Miss A.Vanc (ROM)					
35. Miss N.Llagostera Vives (ESP) & Miss M.Sanchez Lorenzo (ESP)	Miss N.Llagostera Vives & Miss M.Sanchez Lorenzo 6/3 6/1		Miss B.Stewart & Miss S.Stosur [11] 7/6(8) 6/7(5) 6/1		
36. Miss K.Brandi (PUR) & Miss L.Safarova (CZE)					
(WC) 37. Miss K.O'Brien (GBR) & Miss M.South (GBR)	Miss Y.Beygelzimer & Miss A.Serra Zanetti 6/3 6/2	**Miss B.Stewart & Miss S.Stosur [11]** 6/1 6/1			
38. Miss Y.Beygelzimer (UKR) & Miss A.Serra Zanetti (ITA)					
(WC) 39. Miss A.Janes (GBR) & Miss A.Keothavong (GBR)	**Miss B.Stewart & Miss S.Stosur [11]** 6/0 6/3			**Miss B.Stewart & Miss S.Stosur [11]** 3/6 6/4 6/4	
40. **Miss B.Stewart** (AUS) **& Miss S.Stosur** (AUS) **[11]**					
41. **Miss E.Daniilidou** (GRE) **& Miss N.J.Pratt** (AUS) **[14]**	**Miss E.Daniilidou & Miss N.J.Pratt [14]** 7/5 6/4	Miss A.Ivanovic & Miss T.Krizan 6/3 6/1			
42. Mrs K.Peschke (CZE) & Miss J.Schruff (GER)					
43. Miss F.Pennetta (ITA) & Miss F.Schiavone (ITA)	Miss A.Ivanovic & Miss T.Krizan 6/2 6/4		Miss N.Petrova & Miss M.Shaughnessy [4] 6/1 6/3		
44. Miss A.Ivanovic (SCG) & Miss T.Krizan (SLO)					
45. Miss C.Castano (COL) & Miss S.Mamic (CRO)	Miss M.Domachowska & Miss S.Talaja 4/6 6/2 6/2	**Miss N.Petrova & Miss M.Shaughnessy [4]** 6/3 6/1			
46. Miss M.Domachowska (POL) & Miss S.Talaja (CRO)					**Miss C.Black & Mrs L.Huber [2]** 6/3 6/2
(WC) 47. Miss C.Curran (GBR) & Miss N.Grandin (RSA)	**Miss N.Petrova & Miss M.Shaughnessy [4]** 6/4 7/6(3)				
48. **Miss N.Petrova** (RUS) **& Miss M.Shaughnessy** (USA) **[4]**					
49. **Miss D.Hantuchova** (SVK) **& Miss A.Sugiyama** (JPN) **[7]**	**Miss D.Hantuchova & Miss A.Sugiyama [7]** 7/6(1) 6/1	**Miss D.Hantuchova & Miss A.Sugiyama [7]** 7/5 7/6(5)			
(LL) 50. Miss E.Krauth (ARG) & Miss M.Pelletier (CAN)			Miss D.Hantuchova & Miss A.Sugiyama [7] 6/2 6/1		
51. Miss N.Miyagi (JPN) & Miss A.Myskina (RUS)	Miss N.Miyagi & Miss A.Myskina 6/4 6/0				
(WC) 52. Miss A.Hawkins (GBR) & Miss R.Llewellyn (GBR)					
(LL) 53. Miss Y.Fedak (UKR) & Miss L.Osterloh (USA)	Miss J.Russell & Miss M.Santangelo 6/4 6/1	**Miss A.Medina Garrigues & Miss D.Safina [9]** 6/1 7/6(7)			
54. Miss J.Russell (USA) & Miss M.Santangelo (ITA)					
55. Miss S.Karatantcheva (BUL) & Miss T.Tanasugarn (THA)	**Miss A.Medina Garrigues & Miss D.Safina [9]** 6/4 6/2			Miss C.Black & Mrs L.Huber [2] 6/0 6/2	
56. **Miss A.Medina Garrigues** (ESP) **& Miss D.Safina** (RUS) **[9]**					
57. **Miss E.Loit** (FRA) **& Miss B.Strycova** (CZE) **[15]**	**Miss E.Loit & Miss B.Strycova [15]** 6/3 7/5	**Miss E.Loit & Miss B.Strycova [15]** 3/6 6/4 7/5			
58. Miss D.Randriantefy (MAD) & Miss M.Tu (USA)			Miss C.Black & Mrs L.Huber [2] 6/1 7/5		
59. Miss A.Jidkova (RUS) & Miss T.Perebiynis (UKR)	Miss A.Jidkova & Miss T.Perebiynis 6/2 6/1				
60. Miss A.Chakvetadze (RUS) & Miss S.Mirza (IND)					
61. Miss A.Morigami (JPN) & Miss T.Musgrave (AUS)	Miss A.Morigami & Miss T.Musgrave 6/1 7/5	**Miss C.Black & Mrs L.Huber [2]** 6/2 6/1			
(LL) 62. Miss E.Gallovits (ROM) & Miss A.Haynes (USA)					
(WC) 63. Miss S.Borwell (GBR) & Miss E.Webley-Smith (GBR)	**Miss C.Black & Mrs L.Huber [2]** 6/1 6/2				
64. **Miss C.Black** (ZIM) **& Miss L.Huber** (RSA) **[2]**					

Heavy type denotes seeded players. The figure in brackets against names denotes the order in which they were seeded.
(WC)=Wild card. (Q)=Qualifier. (LL)=Lucky loser.

EVENT V: THE MIXED DOUBLES CHAMPIONSHIP 2005

HOLDERS: W. BLACK & MISS C. BLACK

The winners became the holders, for the year only, of the Challenge Cups presented by members of the family of the late Mr S. H. Smith in 1949 and The All England Lawn Tennis and Croquet Club in 2001. The winners received a silver replica of the Challenge Cup. A silver salver was presented to each of the runners-up and a bronze medal to each defeated semi-finalist. The matches were the best of three sets.

First Round	Second Round	Third Round	Quarter-Finals	Semi-Finals	Final
1. B.Bryan (USA) & Miss R.P.Stubbs (AUS) [1]	B.Bryan & Miss R.P.Stubbs [1]				
2. Bye		M.Hood & Miss G.Dulko 6/4 3/6 7/5			
3. A.Pavel (ROM) & Miss A.Vanc (ROM)	M.Hood & Miss G.Dulko 5/7 6/4 11/9		M.Hood & Miss G.Dulko 6/2 6/1		
4. M.Hood (ARG) & Miss G.Dulko (ARG)					
5. P.Pala (CZE) & Miss G.Navratilova (CZE)	G.Oliver & Miss M.Kirilenko 6/3 6/2				
6. G.Oliver (USA) & Miss M.Kirilenko (RUS)		D.Hrbaty & Miss E.Likhovtseva [14] 6/7(6) 6/3 6/2			
7. Bye	D.Hrbaty & Miss E.Likhovtseva [14]				
8. D.Hrbaty (SVK) & Miss E.Likhovtseva (RUS) [14]				P.Hanley & Miss T.Perebiynis 6/3 6/4	
9. J.Palmer (USA) & Miss C.Morariu (USA) [11]	J.Palmer & Miss C.Morariu [11]				
10. Bye		P.Hanley & Miss T.Perebiynis 2/6 6/4 7/5			
(A) 11. P.Hanley (AUS) & Miss T.Perebiynis (UKR)	P.Hanley & Miss T.Perebiynis 6/3 7/6(9)		P.Hanley & Miss T.Perebiynis 6/4 5/2 Ret'd		
12. R.Koenig (RSA) & Miss S.Talaja (CRO)					
13. G.Etlis (ARG) & Miss L.McShea (AUS)	S.Aspelin & Miss S.Mirza 6/7(5) 6/2 7/5				
14. S.Aspelin (SWE) & Miss S.Mirza (IND)		L.Friedl & Miss J.Husarova [7] 6/2 6/4			
15. Bye	L.Friedl & Miss J.Husarova [7]				
16. L.Friedl (CZE) & Miss J.Husarova (SVK) [7]					P.Hanley & Miss T.Perebiynis 6/3 6/4
17. K.Ullyett (ZIM) & Mrs L.Huber (RSA) [4]	K.Ullyett & Mrs L.Huber [4]				
18. Bye		K.Ullyett & Mrs L.Huber [4] walk over			
(WC) 19. A.Parmar (GBR) & Miss J.O'Donoghue (GBR)	M.Kohlmann & Miss A.Myskina 7/5 6/2		K.Ullyett & Mrs L.Huber [4] 4/6 6/3 8/6		
20. M.Kohlmann (GER) & Miss A.Myskina (RUS)					
21. J.Thomas (USA) & Miss J.Russell (USA)	C.Suk & Miss J.Jankovic 1/6 6/4 7/5				
22. C.Suk (CZE) & Miss J.Jankovic (SCG)		A.Ram & Miss C.Martinez [16] walk over			
23. Bye	A.Ram & Miss C.Martinez [16]				
24. A.Ram (ISR) & Miss C.Martinez (ESP) [16]				K.Ullyett & Mrs L.Huber [4] 3/6 6/4 9/7	
25. P.Vizner (CZE) & Miss N.J.Pratt (AUS) [9]	P.Vizner & Miss N.J.Pratt [9]				
26. Bye		T.Parrott & Miss A.Frazier 7/6(3) 6/3			
(WC) 27. R.Barker (GBR) & Miss C.Curran (GBR)	T.Parrott & Miss A.Frazier 3/6 6/3 6/1		M.Bryan & Miss M.Navratilova [5] 7/5 6/7(4) 6/4		
28. T.Parrott (USA) & Miss A.Frazier (USA)					
(WC) 29. A.Murray (GBR) & Miss S.Peer (ISR)	L.Arnold & Miss E.Gagliardi 6/3 6/4				
30. L.Arnold (ARG) & Miss E.Gagliardi (SUI)		M.Bryan & Miss M.Navratilova [5] walk over			
31. Bye	M.Bryan & Miss M.Navratilova [5]				
32. M.Bryan (USA) & Miss M.Navratilova (USA) [5]					
33. T.A.Woodbridge (AUS) & Miss S.Stosur (AUS) [6]	T.A.Woodbridge & Miss S.Stosur [6]				
34. Bye		T.A.Woodbridge & Miss S.Stosur [6] 6/1 7/6(5)			
35. M.Rodriguez (ARG) & Miss A.Jidkova (RUS)	J.Levinsky & Miss A.Chakvetadze 6/2 6/7(5) 8/6		T.A.Woodbridge & Miss S.Stosur [6] 3/6 6/2 6/3		
36. J.Levinsky (CZE) & Miss A.Chakvetadze (RUS)					
37. J.Kerr (AUS) & Miss E.Linetskaya (RUS)	B.MacPhie & Miss A.Spears 6/4 6/4				
(A) 38. B.MacPhie (USA) & Miss A.Spears (USA)		N.Zimonjic & Miss K.Srebotnik [10] 6/2 5/7 6/4			
39. Bye	N.Zimonjic & Miss K.Srebotnik [10]				
40. N.Zimonjic (SCG) & Miss K.Srebotnik (SLO) [10]				J.Bjorkman & Miss L.M.Raymond [3] 6/2 7/6(13)	
41. J.Knowle (AUT) & Miss A-L.Groenefeld (GER) [13]	J.Knowle & Miss A-L.Groenefeld [13]				
42. Bye		J.Knowle & Miss A-L.Groenefeld [13] 6/3 6/7(5) 6/2			
43. J.Erlich (ISR) & Miss B.Stewart (AUS)	J.Erlich & Miss B.Stewart 6/4 6/4		J.Bjorkman & Miss L.M.Raymond [3] 6/2 6/3		
(WC) 44. J.Delgado (GBR) & Miss A.Janes (GBR)					
45. Y.Allegro (SUI) & Miss M.Maleeva (BUL)	A.Lopez Moron & Miss A.Medina Garrigues 7/5 6/2				
46. A.Lopez Moron (ESP) & Miss A.Medina Garrigues (ESP)		J.Bjorkman & Miss L.M.Raymond [3] 6/2 6/1			
47. Bye	J.Bjorkman & Miss L.M.Raymond [3]				
48. J.Bjorkman (SWE) & Miss L.M.Raymond (USA) [3]					M.Bhupathi & Miss M.Pierce 6/4 6/2
49. M.Knowles (BAH) & Miss V.Williams (USA) [8]	M.Knowles & Miss V.Williams [8]				
50. Bye		M.Knowles & Miss V.Williams [8] 6/7(6) 6/4 6/4			
51. J.Gimelstob (USA) & Miss T.Krizan (SLO)	T.Perry & Miss E.S.H.Callens 4/0 Ret'd		O.Rochus & Miss K.Clijsters [12] 3/6 6/3 7/5		
52. T.Perry (AUS) & Miss E.S.H.Callens (BEL)					
53. A.Fisher (AUS) & Miss J.Kostanic (CRO)	A.Fisher & Miss J.Kostanic 6/3 6/4				
54. J.Novak (CZE) & Miss T.Garbin (ITA)		O.Rochus & Miss K.Clijsters [12] 6/1 6/3			
55. Bye	O.Rochus & Miss K.Clijsters [12]				
56. O.Rochus (BEL) & Miss K.Clijsters (BEL) [12]				M.Bhupathi & Miss M.Pierce 6/1 7/5	
57. M.Damm (CZE) & Mrs K.Peschke (CZE) [15]	M.Damm & Mrs K.Peschke [15]				
58. Bye		M.Garcia & Miss M.Santangelo 4/6 6/1 6/2			
59. M.Garcia (ARG) & Miss M.Santangelo (ITA)	M.Garcia & Miss M.Santangelo 6/3 6/4		M.Bhupathi & Miss M.Pierce 6/3 7/6(5)		
60. S.Prieto (ARG) & Mrs M.Vento-Kabchi (VEN)					
61. M.Bhupathi (IND) & Miss M.Pierce (FRA)	M.Bhupathi & Miss M.Pierce 6/3 6/4				
(WC) 62. D.Sherwood (GBR) & Miss E.Baltacha (GBR)		M.Bhupathi & Miss M.Pierce 6/3 6/4			
63. Bye	W.Black & Miss C.Black [2]				
64. W.Black (ZIM) & Miss C.Black (ZIM) [2]					

Heavy type denotes seeded players. The figure in brackets against names denotes the order in which they were seeded.
(A)=Alternates. (WC)=Wild card.

EVENT VI: THE 35 AND OVER GENTLEMEN'S INVITATION DOUBLES 2005
HOLDERS: T.J. MIDDLETON & D. WHEATON

The winners became the holders, for the year only, of a cup presented by The All England Lawn Tennis and Croquet Club. The winners received miniature silver salvers.
A silver medal was presented to each of the runners-up.

GROUP A

GROUP A	T-J. Middleton (USA) & D. Wheaton (USA)	P. Aldrich (RSA) & D. Visser (RSA)	J. Nystrom (SWE) & M. Pernfors (SWE)	S. Davis (USA) & D. Pate (USA)	Wins	Losses
T-J. Middleton (USA) & D. Wheaton (USA)		6/3 6/4 W	7/5 6/3 W	6/7(8) 7/6(4) 6/3 W	3	0
P. Aldrich (RSA) & D. Visser (RSA)	3/6 4/6 L		4/6 4/6 L	3/6 6/3 7/6(4) W	1	2
J. Nystrom (SWE) & M. Pernfors (SWE)	5/7 3/6 L	6/4 6/4 W		3/6 3/6 L	1	2
S. Davis (USA) & D. Pate (USA)	7/6(8) 6/7(4) 3/6 L	6/3 3/6 6/7(4) L	6/3 6/3 W		1	2

GROUP B

GROUP B	J. Hlasek (SUI) & D. Johnson (USA)	S. Casal (ESP) & S. Zivojinovic (SCG)	P. Galbraith (USA) & S. Melville (USA)	G.W. Donnelly (USA) & R. Leach (USA)	Wins	Losses
J. Hlasek (SUI) & D. Johnson (USA)		6/4 6/3 W	6/3 6/3 W	6/7(4) 6/7(4) L	2	1
S. Casal (ESP) & S. Zivojinovic (SCG)	4/6 3/6 L		1/6 6/7(2) L	1/6 5/7 L	0	3
P. Galbraith (USA) & S. Melville (USA)	3/6 3/6 L	6/1 7/6(2) W		6/2 6/7(5) 6/3 W	2	1
G.W. Donnelly (USA) & R. Leach (USA)	7/6(4) 7/6(4) W	6/1 7/5 W	2/6 7/6(5) 3/6 L		2	1

GROUP C

GROUP C	E. Ferreira (RSA) & P. Haarhuis (NED)	L. Jensen (USA) & M. Jensen (USA)	J.B. Fitzgerald (AUS) & M. Kratzmann (AUS)	N. Broad (GBR) & P. Hand (GBR)	Wins	Losses
E. Ferreira (RSA) & P. Haarhuis (NED)		6/2 6/4 W	6/1 6/3 W	walk over W	3	0
L. Jensen (USA) & M. Jensen (USA)	2/6 4/6 L		7/6(4) 5/7 7/6(1) W	7/5 6/3 W	2	1
J.B. Fitzgerald (AUS) & M. Kratzmann (AUS)	1/6 3/6 L	6/7(4) 7/5 6/7(1) L		7/6(1) 6/4 W	1	2
N. Broad (GBR) & P. Hand (GBR)	walk over L	5/7 3/6 L	6/7(1) 4/6 L		0	3

GROUP D

GROUP D	C. Pioline (FRA) & R. Seguso (USA)	J. Frana (ARG) & L. Lavalle (MEX)	A. Jarryd (SWE) & H. Leconte (FRA)	M.J. Bates (GBR) & C. Wilkinson (GBR)	Wins	Losses
C. Pioline (FRA) & R. Seguso (USA)		6/3 7/6(3) W	6/4 4/6 6/3 W	6/3 6/7(4) 6/3 W	3	0
J. Frana (ARG) & L. Lavalle (MEX)	3/6 6/7(3) L		4/6 3/6 L	5/7 6/7(2) L	0	3
A. Jarryd (SWE) & H. Leconte (FRA)	4/6 6/4 3/6 L	6/4 6/3 W		0/6 4/6 L	1	2
M.J. Bates (GBR) & C. Wilkinson (GBR)	3/6 7/6(4) 3/6 L	7/5 7/6(2) W	6/0 6/4 W		2	1

Semi-Final

T-J. Middleton & D. Wheaton
G.W. Donnelly & R. Leach → **T-J. Middleton & D. Wheaton 6/2 6/3**

E. Ferreira & P. Haarhuis
C. Pioline & R. Seguso → **E. Ferreira & P. Haarhuis 6/2 7/5**

Final

T-J. Middleton & D. Wheaton
E. Ferreira & P. Haarhuis → **E. Ferreira & P. Haarhuis 6/3 6/4**

This event was played on a "round robin" basis. Sixteen invited pairs were divided into four groups and each pair in each group played one another. The pairs winning most matches were the winners of their respective groups and played semi-final and final rounds as indicated above. If matches were equal in any group, the head-to-head result between the two pairs with the same number of wins determined the winning pair of the group.
Heavy type denotes seeded players. The matches were the best of three sets. The tie-break operated at six games all in the first two sets.

ALPHABETICAL LIST – 35 AND OVER EVENTS
GENTLEMEN

Aldrich P. (South Africa)
Bates M.J. (Great Britain)
Broad N. (Great Britain)
Casal S. (Spain)
Davis S. (USA)
Donnelly G.W. (USA)
Ferreira E. (South Africa)
Fitzgerald J.B. (Australia)

Frana J. (Argentina)
Galbraith P. (USA)
Haarhuis P. (Netherlands)
Hand P. (Great Britain)
Hlasek J. (Switzerland)
Jarryd A. (Sweden)
Jensen L. (USA)
Jensen M. (USA)

Johnson D. (USA)
Kratzmann M. (Australia)
Lavalle L. (Mexico)
Leach R. (USA)
Leconte H. (France)
Melville S. (USA)
Middleton T.J. (USA)
Nystrom J. (Sweden)

Pate D. (USA)
Pernfors M. (Sweden)
Pioline C. (France)
Seguso R. (USA)
Wheaton D. (USA)
Visser D. (South Africa)
Wilkinson C. (Great Britain)
Zivojinovic S. (Serbia and Mont.)

LADIES

Adams Miss K. (USA)
Arendt Miss N. (USA)
Austin Miss T. (USA)
Bassett-Seguso Mrs C. (USA)
Durie Miss J.M. (Great Britain)
Jausovec Miss M. (Slovenia)
Kloss Miss I. (South Africa)
Magers Mrs G. (USA)

Maleeva Miss K. (Bulgaria)
Mandlikova Miss H. (Australia)
McNeil Miss L. (USA)
Nideffer Mrs R.D. (South Africa)
Novotna Miss J. (Czech Republic)
Smylie Mrs P.D. (Australia)
Tauziat Miss N. (France)
Turnbull Miss W.M. (Australia)

ALPHABETICAL LIST – 45 AND OVER EVENT
GENTLEMEN

Alexander J.G. (Australia)
Amritraj A. (India)
Amritraj V. (India)
Bahrami M. (Iran)
Curren K. (USA)
Davidson O.K. (Australia)
Dowdeswell C. (Great Britain)
Drysdale R. (Great Britain)

Feaver J.W. (Great Britain)
Fleming P. (USA)
Frawley R.J. (Australia)
Gottfried B.E. (USA)
Guenthardt H. (Switzerland)
Gullikson T.R. (USA)
Kriek J. (USA)
Lloyd J.M. (Great Britain)

Mayer A. (USA)
Mayer G. (USA)
McEnroe J.P. (USA)
McNamara P.B. (Australia)
McNamee P. (Australia)
Nastase I. (Romania)
Ramirez R. (Mexico)
Roche A.D. (Australia)

Shiras L. (USA)
Smith S.R. (USA)
Stewart S.E. (USA)
Stockton R.L. (USA)
Stone A. (Australia)
Taroczy B. (Hungary)
Vilas G. (Argentina)
Waltke T. (USA)

EVENT VII: THE 45 AND OVER GENTLEMEN'S INVITATION DOUBLES 2005
HOLDERS: K. CURREN & J. KRIEK

The winners became the holders, for the year only, of a cup presented by The All England Lawn Tennis and Croquet Club.
The winners received miniature silver salvers. A silver medal was presented to each of the runners-up.

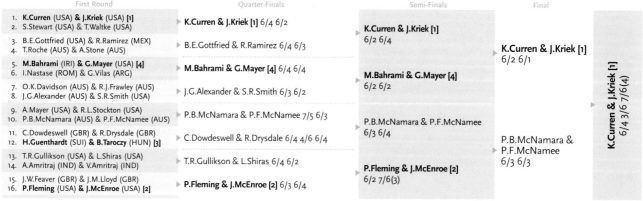

	First Round	Quarter-Finals	Semi-Finals	Final
1.	K.Curren (USA) & J.Kriek (USA) [1]	K.Curren & J.Kriek [1] 6/4 6/2	K.Curren & J.Kriek [1] 6/2 6/4	K.Curren & J.Kriek [1] 6/2 6/1
2.	S.Stewart (USA) & T.Waltke (USA)			
3.	B.E.Gottfried (USA) & R.Ramirez (MEX)	B.E.Gottfried & R.Ramirez 6/4 6/3		
4.	T.Roche (AUS) & A.Stone (AUS)			
5.	M.Bahrami (IRI) & G.Mayer (USA) [4]	M.Bahrami & G.Mayer [4] 6/4 6/4	M.Bahrami & G.Mayer [4] 6/2 6/2	
6.	I.Nastase (ROM) & G.Vilas (ARG)			
7.	O.K.Davidson (AUS) & R.J.Frawley (AUS)	J.G.Alexander & S.R.Smith 6/3 6/2		
8.	J.G.Alexander (AUS) & S.R.Smith (USA)			K.Curren & J.Kriek [1] 6/4 3/6 7/6(4)
9.	A.Mayer (USA) & R.L.Stockton (USA)	P.B.McNamara & P.F.McNamee 7/5 6/3	P.B.McNamara & P.F.McNamee 6/3 6/4	
10.	P.B.McNamara (AUS) & P.F.McNamee (AUS)			
11.	C.Dowdeswell (GBR) & R.Drysdale (GBR)	C.Dowdeswell & R.Drysdale 6/4 4/6 6/4		P.B.McNamara & P.F.McNamee 6/3 6/3
12.	H.Guenthardt (SUI) & B.Taroczy (HUN) [3]			
13.	T.R.Gullikson (USA) & L.Shiras (USA)	T.R.Gullikson & L.Shiras 6/4 6/2	P.Fleming & J.McEnroe [2] 6/2 7/6(3)	
14.	A.Amritraj (IND) & V.Amritraj (IND)			
15.	J.W.Feaver (GBR) & J.M.Lloyd (GBR)	P.Fleming & J.McEnroe [2] 6/3 6/4		
16.	P.Fleming (USA) & J.McEnroe (USA) [2]			

Heavy type denotes seeded players. The figure in brackets against names denotes the order in which they were seeded. The matches were the best of three sets. The tie-break operated at six games all in the first two sets.

EVENT VIII: THE 35 AND OVER LADIES' INVITATION DOUBLES 2005
HOLDERS: MISS M. JAUSOVEC & MISS J. NOVOTNA

The winners became the holders, for the year only, of a cup presented by The All England Lawn Tennis and Croquet Club.
The winners received miniature cups. A silver medal was presented to each of the runners-up.

GROUP A	Miss T. Austin (USA) & Miss J. Novotna (CZE)	Miss I. Kloss (RSA) & Miss K. Maleeva (BUL)	Mrs C. Bassett-Seguso (USA) & Miss M. Jausovec (SLO)	Miss J.M. Durie (GBR) & Miss N. Tauziat (FRA)	Wins	Losses	Final
Miss T. Austin (USA) & Miss J. Novotna (CZE)		6/2 6/0 W	6/0 6/1 W	6/4 2/0 Ret'd W	3	0	Miss T. Austin & Miss J. Novotna
Miss I. Kloss (RSA) & Miss K. Maleeva (BUL)	2/6 0/6 L		6/3 1/6 1/4 Ret'd L	3/6 1/6 L	0	3	
Mrs C. Bassett-Seguso (USA) & Miss M. Jausovec (SLO)	0/6 1/6 L	3/6 6/1 4/1 Ret'd W		1/6 1/6 L	1	2	
Miss J.M. Durie (GBR) & Miss N. Tauziat (FRA)	4/6 0/2 Ret'd L	6/3 6/1 W	6/1 6/1 W		2	1	

GROUP B	Miss L. McNeil (USA) & Mrs P.D. Smylie (AUS)	Mrs G. Magers (USA) & Miss H. Mandlikova (AUS)	Miss N. Arendt (USA) & Miss W.M. Turnbull (AUS)	Miss K. Adams (USA) & Mrs R.D. Nideffer (RSA)	Wins	Losses	Final
Miss L. McNeil (USA) & Mrs P.D. Smylie (AUS)		6/2 7/6(6) W	6/2 6/3 W	3/6 2/6 L	2	1	Miss K. Adams (USA) & Mrs R.D. Nideffer (RSA)
Mrs G. Magers (USA) & Miss H. Mandlikova (AUS)	2/6 6/7(6) L		walk over W	2/6 5/7 L	1	2	
Miss N. Arendt (USA) & Miss W.M. Turnbull (AUS)	2/6 3/6 L	walk over L		7/5 7/5 W	1	2	
Miss K. Adams (USA) & Mrs R.D. Nideffer (RSA)	6/3 6/2 W	6/2 7/5 W	5/7 5/7 L		2	1	

Final: Miss T. Austin & Miss J. Novotna 6/2 6/4

This event was played on a "round robin" basis. Eight invited pairs were divided into 2 groups of 4 and each pair in each group played one another. The pairs winning most matches were the winners of their respective groups and played a final round as indicated above. If matches were equal in any group, the head-to-head result between the two pairs with the same number of wins determined the winning pair of the group. Heavy type denotes seeded players. The matches were the best of three sets. The tie-break operated at six games all in the first two sets.

EVENT IX: THE WHEELCHAIR GENTLEMEN'S DOUBLES 2005

The winners received silver salvers.

Third & Fourth Place Play-off		First Round	Final	
M.Scheffers & R.Vink 7/5 6/3	M.Brychta & L.Majdi	1. M.Jeremiasz (FRA) & J.Mistry (GBR) [1]	M.Jeremiasz & J.Mistry [1] 6/3 6/4	M.Jeremiasz & J.Mistry [1] 4/6 6/3 7/6(3)
		2. M.Brychta (CZE) & L.Majdi (FRA)		
	M.Scheffers & R.Vink	3. M.Scheffers (NED) & R.Vink (NED)	D.Hall & M.Legner [2] 6/2 0/6 6/1	
		4. D.Hall (AUS) & M.Legner (AUT) [2]		

Heavy type denotes seeded players. The figure in brackets against names denotes the order in which they were seeded.

EVENT X: THE BOYS' SINGLES CHAMPIONSHIP 2005
HOLDER: G. MONFILS

The winner became the holder, for the year only, of a cup presented by The All England Lawn Tennis and Croquet Club.
The winner received a miniature cup and the runner-up received a memento. The matches were the best of three sets.

First Round	Second Round	Third Round	Quarter-Finals	Semi-Finals	Final
1. De Bakker, Thiemo [17] (NED)	T.De Bakker [17] 6/2 6/4	T.De Bakker [17] 7/5 4/6 6/1			
(Q) 2. Karpol, Mikhail (CRO)			J.Levine 2/6 7/5 6/4		
3. Roshardt, Robin (SUI)	V.Shokeen 3/6 6/0 6/3				
4. Shokeen, Vivek (IND)				T.Smyczek 6/4 6/3	
5. Dolgopolov, Alexandr (UKR)	J.Levine 6/3 6/2	J.Levine 6/3 3/6 6/4			
6. Levine, Jesse (USA)					R.Haase [14] 7/6(5) 6/7(4) 6/4
7. Sayer, Martin (HKG)	D.Navarrete [16] 6/4 6/4				
8. Navarrete, David [16] (VEN)					
9. Carvalho, Raony [12] (BRA)	I.Sijsling 6/3 6/2	T.Smyczek 6/7(2) 7/6(4) 6/4			
10. Sijsling, Igor (NED)			T.Smyczek 1/6 6/3 6/0		
11. Smyczek, Tim (USA)	T.Smyczek 6/3 6/1				
(LL) 12. Fattar, Anas (MAR)					
(Q) 13. Hodl, Christoph (AUT)	E.Kirillov 6/1 4/6 9/7	N.Desein [6] 7/6(1) 7/5			
14. Kirillov, Evgeny (RUS)					
15. Schottler, Jochen (GER)	N.Desein [6] 7/6(1) 6/0				
16. Desein, Niels [6] (BEL)					
17. Mayer, Leonardo [3] (ARG)	L.Mayer [3] 6/4 5/7 6/4	L.Mayer [3] 6/2 7/6(5)			
(Q) 18. Strydom, Jurgens (NAM)			R.Haase [14] 6/1 7/5		
(Q) 19. Kosler, Jiri (CZE)	M.Shabaz 7/5 7/6(4)				
20. Shabaz, Michael (USA)				R.Haase [14] 7/6(4) 5/7 6/3	
(WC) 21. Khatib, Faris (GBR)	F.Khatib 6/4 7/6(2)	R.Haase [14] 6/3 7/6(5)			
22. Grangeiro, Luis-Henrique (BRA)					
23. Bester, Philip (CAN)	R.Haase [14] 6/4 6/7(3) 6/3				
24. Haase, Robin [14] (NED)					
25. Querrey, Samuel [10] (USA)	S.Querrey [10] 4/6 6/3 6/2	S.Querrey [10] 2/6 6/3 6/1			
(WC) 26. Dickson, Scott (GBR)			M.Cilic [5] 6/4 6/7(1) 6/4		
(Q) 27. Nicholls, Patrick (AUS)	R.Sweeting 7/5 6/4				
28. Sweeting, Ryan (BAH)					
(Q) 29. Koniecko, Bryan (USA)	B.Koniecko 7/5 5/7 6/2	M.Cilic [5] 7/5 6/1			
(WC) 30. Kennaugh, Andrew (GBR)					
31. Sie, Elbert (INA)	M.Cilic [5] 6/3 6/3				
32. Cilic, Marin [5] (CRO)					J.Chardy 6/4 6/3
33. Jelenic, Petar [8] (CRO)	E.Massa 6/4 5/2 Ret'd	J.Chardy 6/3 6/1			
(LL) 34. Massa, Emiliano (ARG)			J.Chardy 6/4 6/4		
35. Tarasevitch, Serguei (BLR)	J.Chardy 7/5 2/6 7/5				
36. Chardy, Jeremy (FRA)				J.Chardy 6/1 6/2	
37. Nedunchezhiya, Jeevan (IND)	M.A.Blake 5/7 6/4 6/1	M.A.Blake 6/4 6/4			
38. Blake, Myles (GBR)					
39. Damico, Kellen (USA)	K.Damico 4/6 6/2 6/4				
40. Miele, Andre [11] (BRA)					
41. Neilly, Timothy [15] (USA)	T.Neilly [15] 6/2 1/6 6/4	T.Neilly [15] 6/2 6/4			
(Q) 42. Nishikori, Kei (JPN)			T.Neilly [15] 6/3 6/1		
43. Arnaboldi, Andrea (ITA)	A.Arnaboldi 7/6(4) 6/7(6) 6/3				
(WC) 44. Taylor, Matthew (GBR)				J.Chardy 6/1 6/2	
45. Coelho, Andrew (AUS)	A.Magdas 7/5 7/5	A.Magdas 7/6(4) 3/6 6/3			
46. Magdas, Abdullah (KUW)					
(Q) 47. Polansky, Peter (CAN)	S-Y.Kim [4] 6/4 6/3				
48. Kim, Sun-Yong Jr. [4] (KOR)					J.Chardy 6/4 7/6(4)
49. Bubka, Sergei [7] (UKR)	D.Lojda 6/4 6/4	D.Lojda 6/4 7/5			
(WC) 50. Lojda, Dusan (CZE)			A.Van Der Duim 6/4 6/2		
51. Thron, Aljoscha (GER)	D.Arnould 7/5 7/6(1)				
52. Arnould, Dylan (USA)				D.Young [2] 6/3 6/2	
53. Singh, Sanam (IND)	S.Singh 6/0 6/2	A.Van Der Duim 6/2 6/3			
(WC) 54. Llewellyn, Christopher (GBR)					
55. Van Der Duim, Antal (NED)	A.Van Der Duim 7/6(10) 3/6 6/2				
56. Ball, Carsten [9] (AUS)					
57. Haider-Maurer, Andreas [13] (AUT)	P.Luisi 6/3 6/3	P.Luisi 6/4 6/4			
58. Luisi, Piero (VEN)			D.Young [2] 7/6(8) 6/2		
59. Sadecky, Alexander (SUI)	A.Sadecky 6/3 6/4				
60. Hunt, Jamie (USA)					
61. Chekhov, Pavel (RUS)	T.Farron-Mahon 6/3 6/3	D.Young [2] 6/1 6/4			
62. Farron-Mahon, Tristan (IRL)					
(WC) 63. Eaton, Chris (GBR)	D.Young [2] 6/1 7/5				
64. Young, Donald [2] (USA)					

EVENT XI: THE BOYS' DOUBLES CHAMPIONSHIP 2005
HOLDERS: B. EVANS & S. OUDSEMA

The winners became the holders, for the year only, of a cup presented by The All England Lawn Tennis and Croquet Club.
The winners received miniature cups and the runners-up received mementoes. The matches were the best of three sets.

First Round	Second Round	Quarter-Finals	Semi-Finals	Final
1. L-H Grangeiro (BRA) & A.Miele (BRA) [9]	R.Haase & I.Sijsling 7/6(4) 6/4	A.Coelho & P.Nicholls 7/6(6) 6/4		
2. R.Haase (NED) & I.Sijsling (NED)			S.Groth & A.Kennaugh 7/6(5) 6/3	
3. A.Coelho (AUS) & P.Nicholls (AUS)	A.Coelho & P.Nicholls 6/3 6/4			
4. P.Chekhov (RUS) & E.Kirillov (RUS)				S.Groth & A.Kennaugh 6/3 3/6 15/13
5. A.Magdas (KUW) & V.Shokeen (IND)	A.Magdas & V.Shokeen 4/6 6/3 9/7	S.Groth & A.Kennaugh 6/3 6/2		
6. C.Hodl (AUT) & J.Schottler (GER)				
(WC) 7. S.Groth (AUS) & A.Kennaugh (GBR)	S.Groth & A.Kennaugh 5/7 6/4 7/5			
8. A.Haider-Maurer (AUT) & D.Lojda (CZE) [5]				
9. A.Arnaboldi (ITA) & N.Desein (BEL) [4]	J.Chardy & D.Navarrete 2/6 6/3 6/4	R.Roshardt & A.Sadecky 6/4 6/3		
10. J.Chardy (FRA) & D.Navarrete (VEN)			T.De Bakker & A.Van Der Duim [6] 6/4 6/4	
11. R.Roshardt (SUI) & A.Sadecky (SUI)	R.Roshardt & A.Sadecky 7/6(4) 6/3			
12. M.A.Blake (GBR) & T.Ley (AUS)				
13. R.Carvalho (BRA) & K.Nishikori (JPN)	R.Carvalho & K.Nishikori 6/3 6/3	T.De Bakker & A.Van Der Duim [6] 3/6 6/2 6/3		
14. E.Sie (INA) & S.Uzawa (JPN)				
15. B.Koniecko (USA) & M.Sayer (HKG)	T.De Bakker & A.Van Der Duim [6] 6/4 6/4			
16. T.De Bakker (NED) & A.Van Der Duim (NED) [6]				
17. E.Massa (ARG) & L.Mayer (ARG) [7]	D.Arnould & J.Hunt 6/1 6/4	C.Llewellyn & J.Strydom 7/6(3) 7/6(5)		
18. D.Arnould (USA) & J.Hunt (USA)			C.Llewellyn & J.Strydom 6/3 7/6(4)	
(A) 19. A.El Sherbini (EGY) & A.Fattar (MAR)	C.Llewellyn & J.Strydom 4/6 7/6(5) 6/4			
(WC) 20. C.Llewellyn (GBR) & J.Strydom (NAM)				J.Levine & M.Shabaz 7/6(4) 6/3
21. P.Jelenic (CRO) & M.Karpol (CRO)	Eaton & F.Khatib 6/4 6/1	K.Damico & T.Smyczek 6/3 6/4		
(WC) 22. C.Eaton (GBR) & F.Khatib (GBR)				
23. K.Damico (USA) & T.Smyczek (USA)	K.Damico & T.Smyczek 4/6 6/3 6/4			
24. S-Y.Kim (KOR) & A.Thron (GER) [3]				
25. P.Luisi (VEN) & R.Sweeting (BAH) [8]	P.Bester & P.Polansky 5/7 6/4 6/4	P.Bester & P.Polansky 7/5 7/6(4)		
26. P.Bester (CAN) & P.Polansky (CAN)			J.Levine & M.Shabaz 5/7 6/4 6/2	
(A) 27. S.Aida (JPN) & J.Kosler (CZE)	J.Nedunchezhiya & S.Singh 6/3 6/4			
28. J.Nedunchezhiya (IND) & S.Singh (IND)				J.Levine & M.Shabaz 6/4 6/1
29. J.Levine (USA) & M.Shabaz (USA)	J.Levine & M.Shabaz 6/3 6/4	J.Levine & M.Shabaz 6/3 6/4		
30. M.Cilic (CRO) & T.Farron-Mahon (IRL)				
31. A.Dolgopolov (UKR) & S.Tarasevitch (BLR)	A.Dolgopolov & S.Tarasevitch 3/6 6/3 6/4			
32. T.Neilly (USA) & S.Querrey (USA) [2]				

Heavy type denotes seeded players. The figure in brackets against names denotes the order in which they were seeded.
(WC)=Wild card. (Q)=Qualifier. (LL)=Lucky loser.

EVENT XII: THE GIRLS' SINGLES CHAMPIONSHIP 2005
HOLDER: MISS K. BONDARENKO

The winner became the holder, for the year only, of a cup presented by The All England Lawn Tennis and Croquet Club.
The winner received a miniature cup and the runner-up received a memento. The matches were the best of three sets.

First Round	Second Round	Third Round	Quarter-Finals	Semi-Finals	Final
1. **Azarenka, Viktoria [1]** (BLR) 2. Pavlovic, Irena (FRA)	**Miss V.Azarenka [1]** 6/2 7/5	**Miss V.Azarenka [1]** 6/3 6/1	**Miss V.Azarenka [1]** 4/6 6/1 6/3	**Miss V.Azarenka [1]** 6/4 6/1	**Miss A.Radwanska** 6/3 6/4
3. Rakhim, Amina (KAZ) 4. Shvedova, Yaroslava (RUS)	Miss A.Rakhim 7/6(5) 4/6 6/2				
5. Tatishvili, Anna (GEO) 6. Sema, Erik (JPN)	Miss A.Tatishvili 6/2 6/4	Miss A.Tatishvili 6/4 6/4			
(WC) 7. Bone, Julia (GBR) 8. **King, Vania [15]** (USA)	**Miss V.King [15]** 6/1 6/2				
9. **Chan, Yung-Jan [9]** (TPE) (Q) 10. Lisicki, Sabine (GER)	**Miss Y-J.Chan [9]** 4/6 6/2 6/0	**Miss Y-J.Chan [9]** 6/1 6/0	Miss D.Cibulkova [5] 6/7(4) 6/4 6/1		
(Q) 11. Revzina, Anastasia (RUS) 12. Gojnea, Madalina (ROM)	Miss M.Gojnea 6/4 7/6(4)				
13. Aziz, Magy (EGY) (LL) 14. Duarte, Ana-Clara (BRA)	Miss M.Aziz 6/2 7/5	**Miss D.Cibulkova [5]** 6/1 6/3			
15. Plotkin, Elizabeth (USA) 16. **Cibulkova, Dominika [5]** (SVK)	**Miss D.Cibulkova [5]** 6/0 6/3				
(WC) 17. **Kirkland, Jessica [3]** (USA) 18. Grebeniuk, Eugenia (RUS)	**Miss J.Kirkland [3]** 6/4 6/2	**Miss J.Kirkland [3]** 6/7(6) 6/4 6/2	Miss J.Kirkland [3] 2/6 6/0 6/2	Miss T.Paszek 6/3 6/1	
(Q) 19. Vermoezen, Aude (BEL) (Q) 20. McDowell, Shayna (AUS)	Miss A.Vermoezen 6/1 6/1				
21. Molinero, Florencia (ARG) (WC) 22. Stoop, Georgie (GBR)	Miss F.Molinero 6/1 7/6(7)	Miss K.Kramperova 6/1 6/0			
23. Kramperova, Katerina (CZE) 24. **Schoofs, Bibiane [16]** (NED)	Miss K.Kramperova 3/6 7/6(2) 6/3				
25. **Erakovic, Marina [11]** (NZL) (WC) 26. Murray, Samantha (GBR)	**Miss M.Erakovic [11]** 6/3 6/0	**Miss M.Erakovic [11]** 6/3 6/3	Miss T.Paszek 6/4 6/2		
27. Rodina, Evgeniya (RUS) 28. Tetreault, Valerie (CAN)	Miss E.Rodina 6/4 6/2				
29. Rebersak, Polona (SLO) 30. Paszek, Tamira (AUT)	Miss T.Paszek 6/2 3/6 6/3	Miss T.Paszek 6/2 6/2			
(Q) 31. Radwanska, Ueszula (POL) 32. **Olaru, Raluca [8]** (ROM)	**Miss R.Olaru [8]** 3/6 6/3 6/4				
33. **Wozniak, Aleksandra [6]** (CAN) 34. Heinser, Jennifer-Lee (USA)	**Miss A.Wozniak [6]** 7/5 6/2	**Miss A.Wozniak [6]** 6/3 6/2	Miss A.Wozniak [6] 5/7 6/4 6/2	Miss A.Radwanska 6/0 4/6 6/2	Miss A.Radwanska 7/5 4/6 6/3
(WC) 35. Curtis, Jade (GBR) 36. Lukasiewicz, Olivia (AUS)	Miss O.Lukasiewicz 6/4 6/3				
37. Kosminskaya, Ekaterina (RUS) 38. Ripoll, Dominice (GER)	Miss E.Kosminskaya 6/1 6/3	Miss N.Frankova 6/4 6/4			
39. Frankova, Nikola (CZE) 40. **Wozniacki, Caroline [10]** (DEN)	Miss N.Frankova 6/3 3/6 6/3				
41. **Niculescu, Monica [14]** (ROM) 42. Alvarez, Maria-Fernanda (BOL)	**Miss M.Niculescu [14]** 6/3 6/1	Miss A.Radwanska 6/0 7/5	Miss A.Radwanska 6/1 7/5		
43. **Radwanska, Agnieszka [POL]** (LL) 44. Dentoni, Corinna (ITA)	Miss A.Radwanska 6/4 6/2				
(WC) 45. Peterzan, Claire (GBR) (Q) 46. Barry, Ellen (NZL)	Miss E.Barry 6/2 6/3	Miss A.Kleybanova 6/0 6/2			
47. Kleybanova, Alisa (RUS) (LL) 48. Nze, Ellah (USA)	Miss A.Kleybanova 6/3 7/6(6)				
49. **Gajdosova, Jarmila [7]** (SVK) 50. Reinhard, Renee (NED)	**Miss J.Gajdosova [7]** 6/2 6/0	**Miss J.Gajdosova [7]** 6/2 6/1	Miss E.Makarova [12] 4/6 7/6(3) 6/0	Miss A.Szavay [2] 6/4 6/4	
(Q) 51. Gaverova, Maya (RUS) (WC) 52. Khan, Natasha (GBR)	Miss N.Khan 6/4 2/6 6/4				
53. Govortsova, Olga (BLR) 54. Buzarnescu, Mihaela (ROM)	Miss M.Buzarnescu 6/4 6/2	**Miss E.Makarova [12]** 7/5 6/4			
(Q) 55. Gloria, Melanie (CAN) 56. **Makarova, Ekaterina [12]** (RUS)	**Miss E.Makarova [12]** 6/2 6/4				
57. **Glatch, Alexa [13]** (USA) 58. Kudryavtseva, Alla (RUS)	**Miss A.Glatch [13]** 5/7 7/6(3) 13/11	**Miss A.Glatch [13]** 4/6 7/5 6/4	Miss A.Szavay [2] 6/4 6/4		
(WC) 59. Peterzan, Laura (GBR) 60. Szatmari, Agnes (ROM)	Miss L.Peterzan 3/6 7/5 6/4				
61. Besser, Astrid (ITA) 62. Sweeting, Jessica (BAH)	Miss A.Besser 7/6(4) 6/3	**Miss A.Szavay [2]** 6/4 5/7 6/1			
63. Morita, Ayumi (JPN) 64. **Szavay, Agnes [2]** (HUN)	**Miss A.Szavay [2]** 6/4 7/6(5)				

EVENT XIII: THE GIRLS' DOUBLES CHAMPIONSHIP 2005
HOLDERS: MISS V. AZARENKA & MISS V. HAVARTSOVA

The winners became the holders, for the year only, of a cup presented by The All England Lawn Tennis and Croquet Club.
The winners received miniature cups and the runners-up received mementoes. The matches were the best of three sets.

First Round	Second Round	Quarter-Finals	Semi-Finals	Final
(A) 1. **Miss V.Azarenka (BLR) & Miss A.Szavay (HUN) [1]** 2. Miss L.Burdette (USA) & Miss A.Weinhold (USA)	**Miss V.Azarenka & Miss A.Szavay [1]** 6/1 6/2	**Miss V.Azarenka & Miss A.Szavay [1]** 4/6 6/1 6/0	Miss V.Azarenka & Miss A.Szavay [1] 6/0 6/1	Miss V.Azarenka & Miss A.Szavay [1] 6/2 6/3
3. Miss E.Kosminskaya (RUS) & Miss A.Kudryavtseva (RUS) 4. Miss A.Radwanska (POL) & Miss U.Radwanska (POL)	Miss A.Radwanska & Miss U.Radwanska 6/4 2/6 6/1			
5. Miss M-F.Alvarez (BOL) & Miss A-C.Duarte (BRA) 6. Miss M.Buzarnescu (ROM) & Miss M.Gojnea (ROM)	Miss M.Buzarnescu & Miss M.Gojnea 6/3 6/0	Miss M.Buzarnescu & Miss M.Gojnea 4/6 6/4 6/1		
7. Miss Y.Hyndman (USA) & Miss J.Stevens (USA) 8. **Miss Y-J.Chan (TPE) & Miss N.Frankova (CZE) [6]**	**Miss Y-J.Chan & Miss N.Frankova [6]** 6/2 6/2			
9. **Miss A.Glatch (USA) & Miss V.King (USA) [8]** 10. Miss O.Govortsova (BLR) & Miss A.Kleybanova (RUS)	Miss O.Govortsova & Miss A.Kleybanova 6/4 5/7 6/4	Miss O.Govortsova & Miss A.Kleybanova 6/4 6/1	Miss O.Govortsova & Miss A.Kleybanova 6/4 6/0	
11. Miss M.Aziz (EGY) & Miss J.Sweeting (BAH) 12. Miss T.Paszek (AUT) & Miss R.Reinhard (NED)	Miss T.Paszek & Miss R.Reinhard 6/4 6/1			
13. Miss F.Molinero (ARG) & Miss I.Pavlovic (FRA) (WC) 14. Miss J.Curtis (GBR) & Miss S.Lisicki (GER)	Miss F.Molinero & Miss I.Pavlovic 6/1 6/4	Miss F.Molinero & Miss I.Pavlovic 6/1 6/2		
15. Miss M.Gloria (CAN) & Miss V.Tetreault (CAN) 16. **Miss D.Cibulkova (SVK) & Miss A.Tatishvili (GEO) [7]**	**Miss D.Cibulkova & Miss A.Tatishvili [7]** 6/3 6/2			
17. **Miss R.Olaru (ROM) & Miss A.Rakhim (KAZ) [5]** 18. Miss A.Besser (ITA) & Miss P.Rebersak (SLO)	**Miss R.Olaru & Miss A.Rakhim [5]** 6/0 6/2	**Miss R.Olaru & Miss A.Rakhim [5]** 4/6 6/4 6/3	Miss B.Schoofs & Miss C.Wozniacki [3] 6/3 3/6 6/2	Miss M.Erakovic & Miss M.Niculescu [2] 6/4 6/4
(WC) 19. Miss C.Peterzan (GBR) & Miss L.Peterzan (GBR) 20. Miss K.Kramperova (CZE) & Miss A.Szatmari (ROM)	Miss K.Kramperova & Miss A.Szatmari 6/3 6/1			
21. Miss E.Nze (USA) & Miss A.Pivovarova (RUS) 22. Miss J.Gajdosova (SVK) & Miss A.Vermoezen (BEL)	Miss J.Gajdosova & Miss A.Vermoezen 6/3 6/2	Miss B.Schoofs & Miss C.Wozniacki [3] 6/1 6/2		
23. Miss E.Makarova (RUS) & Miss E.Rodina (RUS) 24. **Miss B.Schoofs (NED) & Miss C.Wozniacki (DEN) [3]**	**Miss B.Schoofs & Miss C.Wozniacki [3]** 4/6 6/2 7/5			
25. **Miss J-L.Heinser (USA) & Miss E.Plotkin (USA) [8]** (WC) 26. Miss J.Bone (GBR) & Miss S.Murray (GBR)	**Miss J-L.Heinser & Miss E.Plotkin [8]** 6/3 6/3	Miss J-L.Heinser & Miss E.Plotkin [8] 4/6 6/1 6/3	Miss M.Erakovic & Miss M.Niculescu [2] 6/3 6/2	
(WC) 27. Miss N.Khan (GBR) & Miss G.Stoop (GBR) 28. Miss O.Lukaszewicz (AUS) & Miss S.McDowell (AUS)	Miss O.Lukaszewicz & Miss S.McDowell 6/3 6/4			
29. Miss E.Grebeniuk (RUS) & Miss Y.Shvedova (RUS) 30. Miss E.Barry (NZL) & Miss M.Gaverova (RUS)	Miss E.Grebeniuk & Miss Y.Shvedova 6/2 6/4	Miss M.Erakovic & Miss M.Niculescu [2] 6/4 6/2		
31. Miss A.Morita (JPN) & Miss E.Sema (JPN) 32. **Miss M.Erakovic (NZL) & Miss M.Niculescu (ROM) [2]**	**Miss M.Erakovic & Miss M.Niculescu [2]** 6/3 6/3			

Heavy type denotes seeded players. The figure in brackets against names denotes the order in which they were seeded.
(WC)=Wild card. (Q)=Qualifier. (LL)=Lucky loser.

THE CHAMPIONSHIP ROLL GENTLEMEN'S SINGLES
CHAMPIONS AND RUNNERS-UP

1877 S. W. Gore *W. C. Marshall*	**1901** A. W. Gore *R. F. Doherty*	*** 1929** H. Cochet *J. Borotra*	*** 1959** A. Olmedo *R. Laver*	**1983** J. P McEnroe *C. J. Lewis*
1878 P. F. Hadow *S. W. Gore*	**1902** H. L. Doherty *A. W. Gore*	**1930** W. T. Tidlen *W. Allison*	*** 1960** N. A. Fraser *R. Laver*	**1984** J. P McEnroe *J. S. Connors*
* 1879 J. T. Hartley *V. St. L. Gold*	**1903** H. L. Doherty *F. L. Riseley*	*** 1931** S. B. Wood *F. X. Shields*	**1961** R. Laver *C. R. McKinley*	**1985** B. Becker *K. Curren*
1880 J. T. Hartley *H. F. Lawford*	**1904** H. L. Doherty *F. L. Riseley*	**1932** H. E. Vines *H. W. Austin*	**1962** R. Laver *M. F. Mulligan*	**1986** B. Becker *I. Lendl*
1881 W. Renshaw *J. T. Hartley*	**1905** H. L. Doherty *N. E. Brookes*	**1933** J. H. Crawford *H. E. Vines*	*** 1963** C. R. McKinley *F. S. Stolle*	**1987** P. Cash *I. Lendl*
1882 W. Renshaw *E. Renshaw*	**1906** H. L. Doherty *F. L. Riseley*	**1934** F. J. Perry *J. H. Crawford*	**1964** R. Emerson *F. S. Stolle*	**1988** S. Edberg *B. Becker*
1883 W. Renshaw *E. Renshaw*	*** 1907** N. E. Brookes *A. W. Gore*	**1935** F. J. Perry *G. von Cramm*	**1965** R. Emerson *F. S. Stolle*	**1989** B. Becker *S. Edberg*
1884 W. Renshaw *H. F. Lawford*	*** 1908** A. W. Gore *H. Roper Barrett*	**1936** F. J. Perry *G. von Cramm*	**1966** M. Santana *R. D. Ralston*	**1990** S. Edberg *B. Becker*
1885 W. Renshaw *H. F. Lawford*	**1909** A. W. Gore *M. J. G. Ritchie*	*** 1937** J. D. Budge *G. von Cramm*	**1967** J. D. Newcombe *W. P. Bungert*	**1991** M. Stich *B. Becker*
1886 W. Renshaw *H. F. Lawford*	**1910** A. F. Wilding *A. W. Gore*	**1938** J. D. Budge *H. W. Austin*	**1968** R. Laver *A. D. Roche*	**1992** A. Agassi *G. Ivanisevic*
* 1887 H. F. Lawford *E. Renshaw*	**1911** A. F. Wilding *H. Roper Barrett*	*** 1939** R. L. Riggs *E. T. Cooke*	**1969** R. Laver *J. D. Newcombe*	**1993** P. Sampras *J. Courier*
1888 E. Renshaw *H. F. Lawford*	**1912** A. F. Wilding *A. W. Gore*	*** 1946** Y. Petra *G. E. Brown*	**1970** J. D. Newcombe *K. R. Rosewall*	**1994** P. Sampras *G. Ivanisevic*
1889 W. Renshaw *E. Renshaw*	**1913** A. F. Wilding *M. E. McLoughlin*	**1947** J. Kramer *T. Brown*	**1971** J. D. Newcombe *S. R. Smith*	**1995** P. Sampras *B. Becker*
1890 W. J. Hamilton *W. Renshaw*	**1914** N. E. Brookes *A. F. Wilding*	*** 1948** R. Falkenburg *J.E. Bromwich*	*** 1972** S. R. Smith *I. Nastase*	**1996** R. Krajicek *M. Washington*
* 1891 W. Baddeley *J. Pim*	**1919** G. L. Patterson *N. E. Brookes*	**1949** F. R. Schroeder *J. Drobny*	*** 1973** J. Kodes *A. Metreveli*	**1997** P. Sampras *C. Pioline*
1892 W. Baddeley *J. Pim*	**1920** W. T. Tilden *G. L. Patterson*	*** 1950** B. Patty *F. A. Sedgman*	**1974** J. S. Connors *K. R. Rosewall*	**1998** P. Sampras *G. Ivanisevic*
1893 J. Pim *W. Baddeley*	**1921** W. T. Tilden *B. I. C. Norton*	**1951** R. Savitt *K. McGregor*	**1975** A. R. Ashe *J. S. Conners*	**1999** P. Sampras *A. Agassi*
1894 J. Pim *W. Baddeley*	***†1922** G. L. Patterson *R. Lycett*	**1952** F. A. Sedgman *J. Drobny*	**1976** B. Borg *I. Nastase*	**2000** P. Sampras *P. Rafter*
* 1895 W. Baddeley *W. V. Eaves*	*** 1923** W. M. Johnston *F. T. Hunter*	*** 1953** V. Seixas *K. Nielsen*	**1977** B. Borg *J. S. Connors*	**2001** G. Ivanisevic *P. Rafter*
1896 H. S. Mahony *W. Baddeley*	*** 1924** J. Borotra *R. Lacoste*	**1954** J. Drobny *K. R. Rosewall*	**1978** B. Borg *J. S. Connors*	**2002** L. Hewitt *D. Nalbandian*
1897 R. F. Doherty *H. S. Mahony*	**1925** R. Lacoste *J. Borotra*	**1955** T. Trabert *K. Nielsen*	**1979** B. Borg *R. Tanner*	**2003** R. Federer *P. Rafter*
1898 R. F. Doherty *H. L. Doherty*	*** 1926** J. Borotra *H. Kinsey*	*** 1956** L. A Hoad *K. R. Rosewall*	**1980** B. Borg *J. P McEnroe*	**2004** R. Federer *A. Roddick*
1899 R. F. Doherty *A. W. Gore*	**1927** H. Cochet *J. Borotra*	**1957** L. A Hoad *A. J. Cooper*	**1981** J. P McEnroe *B. Borg*	
1900 R. F. Doherty *S. H. Smith*	**1928** R. Lacoste *H. Cochet*	*** 1958** A. J. Cooper *N. A. Fraser*	**1982** J. S. Connors *J. P McEnroe*	

THE CHAMPIONSHIP ROLL LADIES' SINGLES
CHAMPIONS AND RUNNERS-UP

1884	Miss M. Watson	Miss L. Watson
1885	Miss M. Watson	Miss B. Bingley
1886	Miss B. Bingley	Miss M. Watson
1887	Miss L. Dod	Miss B. Bingley
1888	Miss L. Dod	Mrs G. W. Hillyard
* 1889	Mrs G. W. Hillyard	Miss L. Rice
* 1890	Miss L. Rice	Miss M. Jacks
* 1891	Miss L. Dod	Mrs G. W. Hillyard
1892	Miss L. Dod	Mrs G. W. Hillyard
1893	Miss L. Dod	Mrs G. W. Hillyard
* 1894	Mrs G. W. Hillyard	Miss E. L. Austin
* 1895	Miss C. Cooper	Miss H. Jackson
1896	Miss C. Cooper	Mrs. W. H. Pickering
1897	Mrs G. W. Hillyard	Miss C. Cooper
* 1898	Miss C. Cooper	Miss L. Martin
1899	Mrs G. W. Hillyard	Miss C. Cooper
1900	Mrs G. W. Hillyard	Miss C. Cooper
1901	Mrs A. Sterry	Mrs G. W. Hillyard
1902	Miss M. E. Robb	Mrs A. Sterry
* 1903	Miss D. K. Douglass	Miss E. W. Thomson
1904	Miss D. K. Douglass	Mrs A. Sterry
1905	Miss M. Sutton	Miss D. K. Douglass
1906	Miss D. K. Douglass	Miss S. Sutton

1907	Miss S. Sutton	Mrs L. Chambers
* 1908	Mrs A. Sterry	Miss A. M. Morton
* 1909	Miss D. P. Boothby	Miss A. M. Morton
1910	Mrs L. Chambers	Miss D. P. Boothby
1911	Mrs L. Chambers	Miss D. P. Boothby
* 1912	Mrs D. R. Larcombe	Mrs A. Sterry
* 1913	Mrs L. Chambers	Mrs R. J. McNair
1914	Mrs L. Chambers	Mrs D. R. Larcombe
1919	Mlle. S. Lenglen	Mrs L. Chambers
1920	Mlle. S. Lenglen	Mrs L. Chambers
1921	Mlle. S. Lenglen	Miss E. Ryan
† 1922	Mlle. S. Lenglen	Mrs F. Mallory
1923	Mlle. S. Lenglen	Miss K. McKane
1924	Miss K. McKane	Miss H. Wills
1925	Mlle. S. Lenglen	Miss J. Fry
1926	Mrs L. A. Godfree	Sta. L. de Alvarez
1927	Miss H. Wills	Sta. L. de Alvarez
1928	Miss H. Wills	Sta. L. de Alvarez
1929	Miss H. Wills	Miss H. H. Jacobs
1930	Miss F. S. Moody	Miss E. Ryan
* 1931	Fraulein C. Aussem	Fraulein H. Krahwinkel
* 1932	Mrs F. S. Moody	Miss H. H. Jacobs

1933	Mrs F. S. Moody	Miss D. E. Round
* 1934	Miss D. E. Round	Miss H. H. Jacobs
1935	Mrs F. S. Moody	Miss H. H. Jacobs
* 1936	Miss H. H. Jacobs	Frau. S. Sperling
1937	Miss D. E. Round	Miss J. Jedzejowska
1938	Mrs F. S. Moody	Miss H. H. Jacobs
* 1939	Miss A. Marble	Miss K. E. Stammers
1946	Miss P. Betz	Miss L. Brough
* 1947	Miss M. Osborne	Miss D. Hart
1948	Miss L. Brough	Miss D. Hart
1949	Miss L. Brough	Mrs W. du Pont
1950	Miss L. Brough	Mrs W. du Pont
1951	Miss D. Hart	Miss S. Fry
1952	Miss M. Connolly	Miss L. Brough
1953	Miss M. Connolly	Miss D. Hart
1954	Miss M. Connolly	Miss L. Brough
* 1955	Miss L. Brough	Mrs J. G. Fleitz
1956	Miss S. Fry	Miss A. Buxton
* 1957	Miss A Gibson	Miss D. R. Hard
1958	Miss A Gibson	Miss A. Mortimer
* 1959	Miss M. E. Bueno	Miss D. R. Hard
1960	Miss M. E. Bueno	Miss S. Reynolds

1961	Miss A. Mortimer	Miss C. C. Truman
1962	Mrs J. R. Susman	Mrs V. Sukova
* 1963	Miss M. Smith	Miss B. J. Moffitt
1964	Miss M. E. Bueno	Miss M. Smith
1965	Miss M. Smith	Miss M. E. Bueno
1966	Mrs L. W. King	Miss M. E. Bueno
1967	Mrs L. W. King	Mrs P. F. Jones
1968	Mrs L. W. King	Miss J. A. M. Tegart
1969	Mrs P. F. Jones	Mrs L. W. King
* 1970	Mrs B. M. Court	Mrs L. W. King
1971	Miss E. F. Goolagong	Mrs B. M. Court
1972	Mrs L. W. King	Miss E. F. Goolagong
1973	Mrs L. W. King	Miss C. M. Evert
1974	Miss C. M. Evert	Mrs O. Morozovz
1975	Mrs L. W. King	Mrs R. Cawley
* 1976	Miss C. M. Evert	Mrs R. Cawley
1977	Miss S. V. Wade	Miss B. F. Stove
1978	Miss M. Navratilova	Miss C. M. Evert
1979	Miss M. Navratilova	Mrs J. M. Lloyd
1980	Mrs R. Cawley	Mrs J. M. Lloyd
* 1981	Mrs J. M. Lloyd	Miss H. Mandlikova
1982	Miss M. Navratilova	Mrs J. M. Lloyd

1983	Miss M. Navratilova	Miss A. Jaeger
1984	Miss M. Navratilova	Mrs J. M. Lloyd
1985	Miss M. Navratilova	Mrs J. M. Lloyd
1986	Miss M. Navratilova	Miss H. Mandlikova
1987	Miss M. Navratilova	Miss S. Graf
1988	Miss S. Graf	Miss M. Navratilova
1989	Miss S. Graf	Miss M. Navratilova
1990	Miss M. Navratilova	Miss Z. Garrison
1991	Miss S. Graf	Miss G. Sabatini
1992	Miss S. Graf	Miss M. Seles
1993	Miss S. Graf	Miss J. Novotna
1994	Miss C. Martinez	Miss M. Navratilova
1995	Miss S. Graf	Miss A. Sanchez Vicario
1996	Miss S. Graf	Miss A. Sanchez Vicario
* 1997	Miss M. Hingis	Miss J. Novotna
1998	Miss J. Novotna	Miss N. Tauziat
1999	Miss L. A. Davenport	Miss S. Graf
2000	Miss V. Williams	Miss L. A. Davenport
2001	Miss V. Williams	Miss J. Henin
2002	Miss S. Williams	Miss V. Williams
2003	Miss S. Williams	Miss V. Williams
2004	Miss M. Sharapova	Miss S. Williams

MAIDEN NAMES OF LADY CHAMPIONS
(In the tables the following have been recorded in both married and single identities)

Mrs R. Cawley – Miss E. F. Goolagong
Mrs Lambert Chambers – Miss D. K. Douglass
Mrs B. M. Court – Miss M. Smith
Mrs B. C. Covell – Miss P. L. Howkins
Mrs D. E. Dalton – Miss J. A. M. Tegart
Mrs W. du Pont – Miss M. Osborne
Mrs L. A. Godfree – Miss K. McKane
Mrs H. F. Gourlay Cawley – Miss H. F. Gourlay

Mrs G. W. Hillyard – Miss B. Bingley
Mrs P. F. Jones – Miss A. S. Haydon
Mrs L. W. King – Miss B. J. Moffitt
Mrs M. R. King – Miss P. E. Mudford
Mrs D. R. Larcombe – Miss E. W. Thomson
Mrs J. M. Lloyd – Miss C. M. Evert
Mrs F. S. Moody – Miss H. Wills

Mrs O. Morozova – Miss O. Morozova
Mrs L. E. G. Price – Miss S. Reynolds
Mrs G. E. Reid – Miss K. Melville
Mrs P. D. Smylie – Miss E. M. Sayers
Frau S. Sperling – Fraulein H. Krahwinkel
Mrs A. Sterry – Miss C. Cooper
Mrs J. R. Susman – Miss K. Hantze

For the years 1913, 1914 and 1919-1923 inclusive the above records
include the "World's Championships on Grass" granted to The Lawn
Tennis Association by The International Lawn Tennis Federation.
This title was then abolished and commencing in 1924 they
became The Official Lawn Tennis Championships recognised by
The International Lawn Tennis Federation. Prior to 1922 the holders
in the singles events and gentlemen's doubles did not compete in
The Championships but met the winners of these events in the
Challenge Rounds.
† Challenge Round abolished: holders subsequently played through.
* The holder did not defend the title.

THE CHAMPIONSHIP ROLL GENTLEMEN'S DOUBLES

CHAMPIONS AND RUNNERS-UP

1879 L. R. Erskine & H. F. Lawford
F. Durant & G. E. Tabor

1880 W. Renshaw & E. Renshaw
O. E. Woodhouse & C. J. Cole

1881 W. Renshaw & E. Renshaw
W. J. Down & H. Vaughan

1882 J. T. Hartley & R. T. Richardson
J. G. Horn & C. B. Russell

1883 C. W. Grinstead & C. E. Welldon
C. B. Russell & R. T. Milford

1884 W. Renshaw & E. Renshaw
E. W. Lewis & E. L Williams

1885 W. Renshaw & E. Renshaw
C. E. Farrer & A. J. Stanley

1886 W. Renshaw & E. Renshaw
C. E. Farrer & A. J. Stanley

1887 P. Bowes-Lyon & H. W. W. Wilberforce
J. H. Crispe & E. Barratt Smith

1888 W. Renshaw & E. Renshaw
P Bowes-Lyon & H. W. W. Wilberforce

1889 W. Renshaw and E. Renshaw
E. W. Lewis & G. W. Hillyard

1890 J. Pim & F. O. Stoker
E. W. Lewis & G. W. Hillyard

1891 W. Baddeley & H. Baddeley
J. Pim & F. O. Stoker

1892 H. S. Barlow & E. W. Lewis
W. Baddeley & H. Baddeley

1893 J. Pim & F. O. Stoker
E. W. Lewis & H. S. Barlow

1894 W. Baddeley & H. Baddeley
H. S. Barlow & C. H. Martin

1895 W. Baddeley & H. Baddeley
E. W. Lewis & W. V. Eaves

1896 W. Baddeley & H. Baddeley
R. F. Doherty & H. A. Nisbet

1897 R. F. Doherty & H. L. Doherty
W. Baddeley & H. Baddeley

1898 R. F. Doherty & H. L . Doherty
H. A. Nisbet & C. Hobart

1899 R. F. Doherty & H. L. Doherty
H. A. Nisbet & C. Hobart

1900 R. F. Doherty & H. L. Doherty
H. Roper Barrett & H. A. Nisbet

1901 R. F. Doherty & H. L. Doherty
D Davis & H. Ward

1902 S. H. Smith & F. L. Riseley
R. F. Doherty & H. L. Doherty

1903 R. F. Doherty & H. L. Doherty
S. H. Smith & F. L. Riseley

1904 R. F. Doherty & H. L. Doherty
S. H. Smith & F. L. Riseley

1905 R. F. Doherty & H. L. Doherty
S. H. Smith & F. L. Riseley

1906 S. H. Smith & F. L. Riseley
R. F. Doherty & H. L. Doherty

1907 N. E. Brookes & A. F. Wilding
B. C. Wright & K. H. Behr

1908 A. F. Wilding & M. J. G. Ritchie
A. W. Gore & H. Roper Barrett

1909 A. W. Gore & H. Roper Barrett
S. N. Doust & H. A. Parker

1910 A. F. Wilding & M. J. G. Ritchie
A. W. Gore & H. Roper Barrett

1911 M. Decugis & A. H. Gobert
M. J. G. Ritchie & A. F. Wilding

1912 H. Roper Barrett & C. P. Dixon
M. Decugis & A. H. Gobert

1913 H. Roper Barrett & C. P. Dixon
F. W. Rahe & H. Kleinschroth

1914 N. E. Brookes & A. F. Wilding
H. Roper Barrett & C. P. Dixon

1919 R. V. Thomas & P. O'Hara-Wood
R. Lycett & R. W. Heath

1920 R. N. Williams & C. S. Garland
A. R. F. Kingscote & J. C. Parke

1921 R. Lycett & M. Woosnam
F. G. Lowe & A. H. Lowe

1922 R. Lycett & J. O. Anderson
G. L. Patterson & P. O'Hara-Wood

1923 R. Lycett & L. A. Godfree
Count de Gomar & E. Flaquer

1924 F. T. Hunter & V. Richards
R. N. Williams & W. M. Washburn

1925 J. Borotra & R. Lacoste
J. Hennessey & R. Casey

1926 H. Cochet & J. Brugnon
V. Richards & H. Kinsey

1927 F. T. Hunter & W. T. Tilden
J. Brugnon & H. Cochet

1928 H. Cochet & J. Brugnon
G. L. Patterson & J. B. Hawkes

1929 W. Allison & J. Van Ryn
J. C. Gregory & I. G. Collins

1930 W. Allison & J. Van Ryn
J. H. Doeg & G. M. Lott

1931 G. M Lott & J. Van Ryn
H. Cochet & J. Brugnon

1932 J. Borotra & J. Brugnon
G. P. Hughes & F. J. Perry

1933 J. Borotra & J. Brugnon
R. Nunoi & J. Satoh

1934 G. M. Lott & L. R. Stoefen
J. Borotra & J. Brugnon

1935 J. H. Crawford & A. K. Quist
W. Allison & J. Van Ryn

1936 G. P. Hughes & C. R. D. Tuckey
C. E. Hare & F. H. D. Wilde

1937 J. D. Budge & G. Mako
G. P. Hughes & C. R. D. Tuckey

1938 J. D. Budge & G. Mako
H. Henkel & G. von Metaxa

1939 R. L. Riggs & E. T. Cooke
C. E. Hare & F. H. D. Wilde

1946 T. Brown and J. Kramer
G. E. Brown & D. Pails

1947 R. Falkenburg & J. Kramer
A. J. Mottram & O. W. Sidwell

1948 J. E. Bromwich & F. A. Sedgman
T. Brown & G. Mulloy

1949 R. Gonzales & F. Parker
G. Mulloy & F. R. Schroeder

1950 J. E. Bromwich & A. K. Quist
G. E. Brown & O. W. Sidwell

1951 K. McGregor & F. A. Sedgman
J. Drobny & E. W. Sturgess

1952 K. McGregor & F. A. Sedgman
V. Seixas & E. W. Sturgess

1953 L. A. Hoad & K. R. Rosewall
R. N. Hartwig & M. G. Rose

1954 R. N. Hartwig & M. G. Rose
V. Seixas & T. Trabert

1955 R. N. Hartwig & L. A. Hoad
N. A. Fraser & K. R. Rosewall

1956 L. A. Hoad & K. R. Rosewall
N. Pietrangeli & O. Sirola

1957 G. Mulloy & B. Patty
N. A. Fraser & L. A. Hoad

1958 S. Davidson & U. Schmidt
A. J. Cooper & N. A. Fraser

1959 R. Emerson & N. A. Fraser
R. Laver & R. Mark

1960 R. H. Osuna & R. D. Ralston
M. G. Davies & R. K. Wilson

1961 R. Emerson & N. A. Fraser
R. A. J. Hewitt & F. S. Stolle

1962 R. A. J. Hewitt & F. S. Stolle
B. Jovanovic & N. Pilic

1963 R. H. Osuna & A. Palafox
J. C. Barclay & P. Darmon

1964 R. A. J. Hewitt & F. S. Stolle
R. Emerson & K. N. Fletcher

1965 J. D. Newcombe & A. D. Roche
K. N. Fletcher & R. A. J. Hewitt

1966 K. N. Fletcher & J. D. Newcombe
W. W. Bowrey & O. K. Davidson

1967 R. A. J. Hewitt & F. D. McMillan
R. Emerson & K. N. Fletcher

1968 J. D. Newcombe & A. D. Roche
K. R. Rosewall & F. S. Stolle

1969 J. D. Newcombe & A. D. Roche
T. S. Okker & M. C. Reissen

1970 J. D. Newcombe & A. D. Roche
K. R. Rosewall & F. S. Stolle

1971 R. S. Emerson & R. G. Laver
A. R. Ashe & R. D. Ralston

1972 R. A. J. Hewitt & F. D. McMillan
S. R. Smith & E. J. van Dillen

1973 J. S. Connors & I. Nastase
J. R. Cooper & N. A. Fraser

1974 J. D. Newcombe & A. D. Roche
R. C. Lutz & S. R. Smith

1975 V. Gerulaitis & A. Mayer
C. Dowdeswell & A. J. Stone

1976 B. E. Gottfried & R. Ramirez
R. L. Case & G. Masters

1977 R. L. Case & G. Masters
J. G. Alexander & P. C. Dent

1978 R. A. J. Hewitt & F. D. McMillan
P. Fleming & J. P. McEnroe

1979 P. Fleming & J. P. McEnroe
B. E. Gottfried & R. Ramirez

1980 P. McNamara & P. McNamee
R. C. Lutz & S. R. Smith

1981 P. Fleming & J. P. McEnroe
R. C. Lutz & S. R. Smith

1982 P. McNamara & P. McNamee
P. Fleming & J. P. McEnroe

1983 P. Fleming & J. P. McEnroe
T. E. Gullikson & T. R. Gullikson

1984 P. Fleming & J. P. McEnroe
P. Cash & P. McNamee

1985 H. P. Guenthardt & B. Taroczy
P. Cash & J. B. Fitzgerald

1986 J. Nystrom & M. Wilander
G. Donnelly & P. Fleming

1987 K. Flach & R. Seguso
S. Casal & E. Sanchez

1988 K. Flach & R. Seguso
J. B. Fitzgerald & A. Jarryd

1989 J. B. Fitzgerald & A. Jarryd
R. Leach & J. Pugh

1990 R. Leach & J. Pugh
P. Aldrich & D. T. Visser

1991 J. B. Fitzgerald & A. Jarryd
J. Frana & L. Lavalle

1992 J. P. McEnroe & M. Stich
J. Grabb & R. A. Reneberg

1993 T. A. Woodbridge & M. Woodforde
G. Connell & P. Galbraith

1994 T. A. Woodbridge & M. Woodforde
G. Connell & P. Galbraith

1995 T. A. Woodbridge & M. Woodforde
R. Leach & S. Melville

1996 T. A. Woodbridge & M. Woodforde
B. Black & G. Connell

1997 T. A. Woodbridge & M. Woodforde
J. Eltingh & P. Haarhuis

1998 J. Eltingh & P. Haarhuis
T. A. Woodbridge & M. Woodforde

1999 M. Bhupathi & L. Paes
P. Haarhuis & J. Palmer

2000 T. A. Woodbridge & M. Woodforde
P. Haarhuis & S. Stolle

2001 D. Johnson & J. Palmer
J. Novak & D. Rikl

2002 J. Bjorkman & T. A Woodbridge
M. Knowles & D. Nestor

2003 J. Bjorkman & T. A Woodbridge
M. Bhupathi & M. Mirnyi

2004 J. Bjorkman & T. A Woodbridge
J. Knowle & N. Zimonjic

THE CHAMPIONSHIP ROLL LADIES' DOUBLES

CHAMPIONS AND RUNNERS-UP

1913 Mrs R. J. McNair & Miss D. P. Boothby
Mrs A. Sterry & Mrs. Lambert Chambers

1914 Miss E. Ryan & Miss A. M. Morton
Mrs D. R. Larcombe & Mrs. F. J. Hannam

1919 Mlle S. Lenglen & Miss E. Ryan
Mrs Lambert Chambers & Mrs. D. R. Larcombe

1920 Mlle S. Lenglen & Miss E. Ryan
Mrs Lambert Chambers & Mrs. D. R. Larcombe

1921 Mlle S. Lenglen & Miss E. Ryan
Mrs A. E. Beamish & Mrs. G. E. Peacock

1922 Mlle S. Lenglen & Miss E. Ryan
Mrs A. D. Stocks & Miss K. McKane

1923 Mlle S. Lenglen & Miss E. Ryan
Miss J. Austin & Miss E. L. Colyer

1924 Mrs H. Wightman & Miss H. Wills
Mrs B. C. Covell & Miss K. McKane

1925 Mlle S. Lenglen & Miss E. Ryan
Mrs A. V. Bridge & Mrs. C. G. McIlquham

1926 Miss E. Ryan & Miss M. K. Browne
Mrs L. A. Godfree & Miss E. L. Colyer

1927 Miss H. Wills & Miss E. Ryan
Miss E. L. Heine & Mrs. G. E. Peacock

1928 Mrs Holcroft-Watson & Miss P. Saunders
Miss E. H. Harvey & Miss E. Bennett

1929 Mrs Holcroft-Watson & Mrs. L.R.C. Michell
Mrs B. C. Covell & Mrs. D. C. Shepherd-Barron

1930 Mrs F. S. Moody & Miss E. Ryan
Miss E. Cross & Miss S. Palfrey

1931 Mrs D.C. Shepherd-Barron & Miss P.E. Mudford
Mlle D. Metaxa & Mlle. J. Sigart

1932 Mlle D. Metaxa & Mlle. J. Sigart
Miss E. Ryan & Miss H. H. Jacobs

1933 Mme R. Mathieu & Miss E. Ryan
Miss F. James & Miss A. M. Yorke

1934 Mme R. Mathieu & Miss E. Ryan
Mrs D. Andrus & Mme. S. Henrotin

1935 Miss F. James & Miss K. E. Stammers
Mme R. Mathieu & Frau. S. Sperling

1936 Miss F. James & Miss K. E. Stammers
Mrs S. P. Fabyan & Miss H. H. Jacobs

1937 Mme R. Mathieu & Miss A. M. Yorke
Mrs M. R. King & Mrs. J. B. Pittman

1938 Mrs S. P. Fabyan & Miss A. Marble
Mme R. Mathieu & Miss A. M. Yorke

1939 Mrs S. P. Fabyan & Miss A. Marble
Miss H. H. Jacobs & Miss A. M. Yorke

1946 Miss L. Brough & Miss M. Osborne
Miss P. Betz & Miss D. Hart

1947 Miss D. Hart & Mrs. P. C. Todd
Miss L. Brough & Miss M. Osborne

1948 Miss L. Brough & Mrs. W. du Pont
Miss D. Hart & Mrs. P. C. Todd

1949 Miss L. Brough & Mrs. W. du Pont
Miss G. Moran & Mrs. P. C. Todd

1950 Miss L. Brough & Mrs. W. du Pont
Miss S. Fry & Miss D. Hart

1951 Miss S. Fry & Miss D. Hart
Miss L. Brough & Mrs. W. du Pont

1952 Miss S. Fry & Miss D. Hart
Miss L. Brough & Miss M. Connolly

1953 Miss S. Fry & Miss D. Hart
Miss M. Connolly & Miss J. Sampson

1954 Miss L. Brough & Mrs. W. du Pont
Miss S. Fry & Miss D. Hart

1955 Miss A. Mortimer & Miss J. A. Shilcock
Miss S. J. Bloomer & Miss P. E. Ward

1956 Miss A. Buxton & Miss A. Gibson
Miss F. Muller & Miss D. G. Seeney

1957 Miss A. Gibson & Miss D. R. Hard
Mrs K. Hawton & Mrs. T. D. Long

1958 Miss M. E. Bueno & Miss A. Gibson
Mrs W. du Pont & Miss M. Varner

1959 Miss J. Arth & Miss D. R. Hard
Mrs J. G. Fleitz & Miss C. C. Truman

1960 Miss M. E. Bueno & Miss D. R. Hard
Miss S. Reynolds and Miss R. Schuurman

1961 Miss K. Hantze & Miss B. J. Moffitt
Miss J. Lehane & Miss M. Smith

1962 Miss B. J. Moffitt & Mrs. J. R. Susman
Mrs L. E. G. Price & Miss R. Schuurman

1963 Miss M. E. Bueno & Miss D. R. Hard
Miss R. A. Ebbern & Miss M. Smith

1964 Miss M. Smith & Miss L. R. Turner
Miss B. J. Moffitt & Mrs. J. R. Susman

1965 Miss M. E. Bueno & Miss B. J. Moffitt
Miss F. Durr & Miss J. LieVrig

1966 Miss M. E. Bueno & Miss N. Richey
Miss M. Smith & Miss J. A. M. Tegart

1967 Miss R. Casals & Mrs. L. W. King
Miss M. E. Bueno & Miss N. Richey

1968 Miss R. Casals & Mrs. L. W. King
Miss F. Durr & Mrs. P. F. Jones

1969 Mrs B. M. Court & Miss J. A. M. Tegart
Miss P. S. A. Hogan & Miss M. Michel

1970 Miss R. Casals & Mrs. L. W. King
Miss F. Durr & Miss S. V. Wade

1971 Miss R. Casals & Mrs. L. W. King
Mrs B. M. Court & Miss E. F. Goolagong

1972 Mrs L. W. King & Miss B. F. Stove
Mrs D. E. Dalton & Miss F. Durr

1973 Miss R. Casals & Mrs. L. W. King
Miss F. Durr & Miss B. F. Stove

1974 Miss E. F. Goolagong & Miss M. Michel
Miss H. F. Gourlay & Miss K. M. Krantzcke

1975 Miss A. Kiyomura & Miss K. Sawamatsu
Miss F. Durr & Miss B. F. Stove

1976 Miss C. M. Evert & Miss M. Navratilova
Mrs L. W. King & Miss B. F. Stove

1977 Mrs H. F. Gourlay Cawley & Miss J. C. Russell
Miss M. Navratilova & Miss B. F . Stove

1978 Mrs G. E. Reid & Miss. W. M. Turnbull
Miss M. Jausovec & Miss V. Ruzici

1979 Mrs L. W. King & Miss M. Navratilova
Miss B. F. Stove & Miss W. M. Turnbull

1980 Miss K. Jordan & Miss A. E. Smith
Miss R. Casals & Miss W. M. Turnbull

1981 Miss M. Navratilova & Miss P. H. Shriver
Miss K. Jordan & Miss A. E. Smith

1982 Miss M. Navratilova & Miss P. H. Shriver
Miss K. Jordan & Miss A. E. Smith

1983 Miss M. Navratilova & Miss P. H. Shriver
Miss R. Casals & Miss W. M. Turnbull

1984 Miss M. Navratilova & Miss P. H. Shriver
Miss K. Jordan & Miss A. E. Smith

1985 Miss K. Jordan & Mrs. P. D. Smylie
Miss M. Navratilova & Miss P. H. Shriver

1986 Miss M. Navratilova & Miss P. H. Shriver
Miss H. Mandlikova & Miss W. M. Turnbull

1987 Miss C. Kohde-Kilsch & Miss H. Sukova
Miss B. Nagelsen & Mrs. P. D. Smylie

1988 Miss S. Graf & Miss G. Sabatini
Miss L. Savchenko & Miss N. Zvereva

1989 Miss J. Novotna & Miss H. Sukova
Miss L. Savchenko & Miss N. Zvereva

1990 Miss J. Novotna & Miss H. Sukova
Miss K. Jordan & Mrs. P. D. Smylie

1991 Miss L. Savchenko & Miss N. Zvereva
Miss G. Fernandez & Miss J. Novotna

1992 Miss G. Fernandez & Miss N. Zvereva
Miss J. Novotna & Mrs. L. Savchenko-Neiland

1993 Miss G. Fernandez & Miss N. Zvereva
Mrs L. Neiland & Miss J. Novotna

1994 Miss G. Fernandez & Miss N. Zvereva
Miss J. Novotna & Miss A. Sanchez Vicario

1995 Miss J. Novotna & Miss A. Sanchez Vicario
Miss G. Fernandez & Miss N. Zvereva

1996 Miss M. Hingis & Miss H. Sukova
Miss M.J. McGrath & Mrs. L. Neiland

1997 Miss G. Fernandez & Miss N. Zvereva
Miss N.J. Arendt & Miss M.M. Bollegraf

1998 Miss M. Hingis and Miss J. Novotna
Miss L.A. Davenport & Miss N. Zvereva

1999 Miss L.A. Davenport & Miss C. Morariu
Miss M. de Swardt & Miss E. Tatarkova

2000 Miss S. Williams & Miss V. Williams
Mrs J. Halard–Decugis & Miss A. Sugiyama

2001 Miss L.M. Raymond & Miss R.P. Stubbs
Miss K. Clijsters & Miss A. Sugiyama

2002 Miss S. Williams & Miss V. Williams
Miss V. Ruano Pascual & Miss P. Suarez

2003 Miss K. Clijsters & Miss A. Sugiyama
Miss V. Ruano Pascual & Miss P. Suarez

2004 Miss C. Black & Miss R.P. Stubbs
Mrs L. Huber & Miss A. Sugiyama

THE CHAMPIONSHIP ROLL

JUNIOR BOYS SINGLES CHAMPIONS AND RUNNERS-UP

1947	K. Nielsen (Denmark) *S. V. Davidson (Sweden)*	1959	T. Lejus (U.S.S.R.) *R. W. Barnes (Brazil)*	1971	R. Kreiss (U.S.A.) *S. A. Warboys (G.B.)*	1983	S. Edberg (Sweden) *J. Frawley (Australia)*	1994	S. Humphries (U.S.A.) *M. A. Philippoussis (Australia)*
1948	S. Stockenberg (Sweden) *D. Vad (Hungary)*	1960	A. R. Mandelstam (S.A.) *J. Mukerjea (India)*	1972	B. Borg (Sweden) *C. J. Mottram (G.B.)*	1984	M.Kratzmann (Australia) *S. Kruger (S.A.)*	1995	O. Mutis (France) *N. Kiefer (Germany)*
1949	S. Stockenberg (Sweden) *J. A. T. Horn (G.B.)*	1961	C. E. Graebner (U.S.A.) *E. Blanke (Austria)*	1973	W. Martin (U.S.A.) *C. S. Dowdeswell (Rhodesia)*	1985	L. Lavalle (Mexico) *E. Velez (Mexico)*	1996	V. Voltchkov (Belarus) *I. Ljubicic (Croatia)*
1950	J. A. T. Horn (G.B.) *K. Mobarek (Egypt)*	1962	S. Matthews (G.B.) *A. Metreveli (U.S.S.R.)*	1974	W. Martin (U.S.A.) *A. Amritraj (India)*	1986	E. Velez (Mexico) *J. Sanchez (Spain)*	1997	W. Whitehouse (S.A.) *D. Elsner (Germany)*
1951	J. Kupferburger (S.A.) *K. Mobarek (Egypt)*	1963	N. Kalogeropoulos (Greece) *I. El Shafei (U.A.R.)*	1975	C. J. Lewis (N.Z.) *R. Ycaza (Ecuador)*	1987	D. Nargiso (Italy) *J. R. Stoltenberg (Australia)*	1998	R. Federer (Switzerland) *I. Labadze (Georgia)*
1952	R. K. Wilson (G.B.) *T. T. Fancutt (S.A.)*	1964	I. El Shafei (U.A.R.) *V. Korotkov (U.S.S.R.)*	1976	H. Guenthardt (Switzerland) *P. Elter (Germany)*	1988	N. Pereira (Venezuela) *G. Raoux (France)*	1999	J. Melzer (Austria) *K. Pless (Denmark)*
1953	W. A. Knight (G.B.) *R. Krishnan (India)*	1965	V. Korotkov (U.S.S.R.) *G. Goven (France)*	1977	V. A. Winitsky (U.S.A.) *T. E. Teltscher (U.S.A.)*	1989	N. Kulti (Sweden) *T. A. Woodbridge (Australia)*	2000	N. Mahut (France) *M. Ancic (Croatia)*
1954	R. Krishnan (India) *A. J. Cooper (Australia)*	1966	V. Korotkov (U.S.S.R.) *B. E. Fairlie (N.Z.)*	1978	I. Lendl (Czechoslovakia) *J. Turpin (U.S.A.)*	1990	L. Paes (India) *M. Ondruska (S.A.)*	2001	R. Valent (Switzerland) *G. Muller (Luxembourg)*
1955	M. P. Hann (G.B.) *J. E. Lundquist (Sweden)*	1967	M. Orantes (Spain) *M. S. Estep (U.S.A.)*	1979	R. Krishnan (India) *D. Siegler (U.S.A.)*	1991	T. Enquist (Sweden) *M. Joyce (U.S.A.)*	2002	T. Reid (Australia) *L. Quahab (Algeria)*
1956	R. Holmberg (U.S.A.) *R. G. Laver (Australia)*	1968	J. G. Alexander (Australia) *J. Thamin (France)*	1980	T. Tulasne (France) *H. D. Beutel (Germany)*	1992	D. Skoch (Czechoslovakia) *B. Dunn (U.S.A.)*	2003	F. Mergea (Romania) *C. Guccione (Australia)*
1957	J. I. Tattersall (G.B.) *I. Ribeiro (Brazil)*	1969	B. Bertram (S.A.) *J. G. Alexander (Australia)*	1981	M. W. Anger (U.S.A.) *P. Cash (Australia)*	1993	R. Sabau (Romania) *J. Szymanski (Venezuela)*	2004	G. Monfils (France) *M. Kasiri (G.B.)*
1958	E. Buchholz (U.S.A.) *P. J. Lall (India)*	1970	B. Bertram (S.A.) *F. Gebert (Germany)*	1982	P. Cash (Australia) *H. Sundstrom (Sweden)*				

JUNIOR BOYS DOUBLES CHAMPIONS AND RUNNERS-UP

1982	P. Cash & J. Frawley *R. D. Leach & J. J. Ross*	1987	J. Stoltenberg & T. Woodbridge *D. Nargiso & E. Rossi*	1992	S. Baldas & S. Draper *M. S. Bhupathi & N. Kirtane*	1997	L. Horna & N. Massu *J. Van de Westhuizen & W. Whitehouse*	2001	F. Dancevic & G. Lapentti *B. Echagaray & S. Gonzales*
1983	M. Kratzmann & S. Youl *M. Nastase & O. Rahnasto*	1988	J. Stoltenberg & T. Woodbridge *D. Rikl & T. Zdrazila*	1993	S. Downs & J. Greenhalgh *N. Godwin & G. Williams*	1998	R. Federer & O. Rochus *M. Llodra & A. Ram*	2002	F. Mergea & H. Tecau *B. Baker & B. Ram*
1984	R. Brown & R. Weiss *M. Kratzmann & J. Svensson*	1989	J. Palmer & J. Stark *J-L. De Jager & W. R. Ferreira*	1994	B. Ellwood & M. Philippoussis *V. Platenik & R. Schlachter*	1999	G. Coria & D. Nalbandian *T. Enev & J. Nieminem*	2003	F. Mergea & H. Tecau *A. Feeney & C. Guccione*
1985	A. Moreno & J. Yzaga *P. Korda & C. Suk*	1990	S. Lareau & S. Leblanc *C. Marsh & M. Ondruska*	1995	M. Lee & J.M. Trotman *A. Hernandez & M. Puerta*	2000	D. Coene & K. Vliegen *A. Banks & B. Riby*	2004	B. Evans & S. Oudsema *R. Haase & V. Troicki*
1986	T. Carbonell & P. Korda *S. Barr & H. Karrasch*	1991	K. Alami & G. Rusedski *J-L. De Jager & A. Medvedev*	1996	D. Bracciali & J. Robichaud *D. Roberts & W. Whitehouse*				

JUNIOR GIRLS SINGLES CHAMPIONS AND RUNNERS-UP

1947	Miss G. Domken (Belgium) *Miss B. Wallen (Sweden)*	1962	Miss G. Baksheeva (U.S.S.R.) *Miss E. P. Terry (N.Z.)*	1977	Miss L. Antonoplis (U.S.A.) *Miss Mareen Louie (U.S.A.)*	1991	Miss B. Rittner (Germany) *Miss E. Makarova (U.S.S.R.)*
1948	Miss O. Miskova (Czechoslovakia) *Miss V. Rigollet (Switzerland)*	1963	Miss D. M. Salfati (France) *Miss K. Dening (Australia)*	1978	Miss T. Austin (U.S.A.) *Miss H. Mandlikova (Czechoslovakia)*	1992	Miss C. Rubin (U.S.A.) *Miss L. Courtois (Belgium)*
1949	Miss C. Mercelis (Belgium) *Miss J. S. V. Partridge (G.B.)*	1964	Miss P. Bartkowicz (U.S.A.) *Miss A. E. Subirats (Mexico)*	1979	Miss M. L. Piatek (U.S.A.) *Miss A. A. Moulton (U.S.A.)*	1993	Miss N. Feber (Belgium) *Miss R. Grande (Italy)*
1950	Miss L. Cornell (G.B.) *Miss A. Winter (Norway)*	1965	Miss O. Morozova (U.S.S.R.) *Miss R. Giscarfe (Argentina)*	1980	Miss D. Freeman (Australia) *Miss S. J. Leo (Australia)*	1994	Miss M. Hingis (Switzerland) *Miss M-R. Jeon (Korea)*
1951	Miss L. Cornell (G.B.) *Miss S. Lazzarino (Italy)*	1966	Miss B. Lindstrom (Finland) *Miss J. A. Congdon (G.B.)*	1981	Miss Z. Garrison (U.S.A.) *Miss R. R. Uys (S.A.)*	1995	Miss A. Olsza (Poland) *Miss T. Tanasugarn (Thailand)*
1952	Miss F. J. I. ten Bosch (Netherlands) *Miss R. Davar (India)*	1967	Miss J. Salome (Netherlands) *Miss E. M. Strandberg (Sweden)*	1982	Miss C. Tanvier (France) *Miss H. Sukova (Czechoslovakia)*	1996	Miss A. Mauresmo (France) *Miss M. L. Serna (Spain)*
1953	Miss D. Kilian (S.A.) *Miss V. A. Pitt (G.B.)*	1968	Miss K. Pigeon (U.S.A.) *Miss L. E. Hunt (Australia)*	1983	Miss P. Paradis (France) *Miss P. Hy (Hong Kong)*	1997	Miss C. Black (Zimbabwe) *Miss A. Rippner (U.S.A.)*
1954	Miss V. A. Pitt (G.B.) *Miss C. Monnot (France)*	1969	Miss K. Sawamatsu (Japan) *Miss B. I. Kirk (S.A.)*	1984	Miss A. N. Croft (G.B.) *Miss E. Reinach (S.A.)*	1998	Miss K. Srebotnik (Slovenia) *Miss K. Clijsters (Belgium)*
1955	Miss S. M. Armstrong (G.B.) *Miss B. de Chambure (France)*	1970	Miss S. Walsh (U.S.A) *Miss M. V. Kroschina (U.S.S.R.)*	1985	Miss A. Holikova (Czechoslovakia) *Miss J. M. Byrne (Australia)*	1999	Miss I. Tulyagnova (Uzbekhistan) *Miss L. Krasnoroutskaya (Russia)*
1956	Miss A. S. Haydon (G.B.) *Miss I. Buding (Germany)*	1971	Miss M.V. Kroschina (U.S.S.R.) *Miss S. H. Minford (G.B.)*	1986	Miss N.M. Zvereva (U.S.S.R.) *Miss L. Meskhi (U.S.S.R.)*	2000	Miss M. E. Salerni (Argentina) *Miss T. Perebiynis (Ukraine)*
1957	Miss M. Arnold (U.S.A.) *Miss E. Reyes (Mexico)*	1972	Miss I. Kloss (S.A.) *Miss G. L. Coles (G.B.)*	1987	Miss N.M. Zvereva (U.S.S.R.) *Miss J. Halard (France)*	2001	Miss A. Widjaja (Indonesia) *Miss D. Safina (Russia)*
1958	Miss S. M. Moore (U.S.A.) *Miss A. Dmitrieva (U.S.S.R.)*	1973	Miss A. Kiyomura (U.S.A.) *Miss M. Navratilova (Czechoslovakia)*	1988	Miss B. Schultz (Netherlands) *Miss E. Derly (France)*	2002	Miss V. Douchevina (Russia) *Miss M. Sharapova (Russia)*
1959	Miss J. Cross (S.A.) *Miss D. Schuster (Austria)*	1974	Miss M. Jausovec (Yugoslavia) *Miss M. Simionescu (Romania)*	1989	Miss A. Strnadova (Czechoslovakia) *Miss M. J. McGrath (U.S.A.)*	2003	Miss K. Flipkens (Belgium) *Miss A. Tchakvetadze (Russia)*
1960	Miss K. Hantze (U.S.A.) *Miss L. M Hutchings (S.A.)*	1975	Miss N.Y. Chmyreva (U.S.S.R.) *Miss R. Marsikova (Czechoslovakia)*	1990	Miss A. Strnadova (Czechoslavakia) *Miss K. Sharpe (Australia)*	2004	Miss K. Bondarenko (Ukraine) *Miss A. Ivanovic (Serbia and Montenegro)*
1961	Miss G. Baksheeva (U.S.S.R.) *Miss K. D. Chabot (U.S.A.)*	1976	Miss N. Y. Chmyreva (U.S.S.R.) *Miss M. Kruger (S.A.)*				

JUNIOR GIRLS DOUBLES CHAMPIONS AND RUNNERS-UP

1982	Miss B. Herr & Miss P. Barg *Miss B. S. Gerken & Miss G. A. Rush*	1988	Miss J. A. Faull & Miss R. McQuillan *Miss A. Dechaume & Miss E. Derly*	1994	Miss E. De Villiers & Miss E. E. Jelfs *Miss C. M. Morariu & Miss L. Varmuzova*	2000	Miss I. Gaspar & Miss T. Perebiynis *Miss D. Bedanova & Miss M. E. Salerni*
1983	Miss P. Fendick & Miss P. Hy *Miss C. Anderholm & Miss H. Olsson*	1989	Miss J. Capriati & Miss M. McGrath *Miss A. Strnadova & Miss E. Sviglerova*	1995	Miss C. Black & Miss A. Olsza *Miss T. Musgrove & Miss J. Richardson*	2001	Miss G. Dulko & Miss A. Harkleroad *Miss C. Horiatopoulos & Miss B. Mattek*
1984	Miss C. Kuhlman & Miss S. Rehe *Miss V. Milvidskaya & Miss L. I. Savchenko*	1990	Miss K. Habsudova & Miss A. Strnadova *Miss N. J. Pratt & Miss K. Sharpe*	1996	Miss O. Barabanschikova & Miss A. Mauresmo *Miss L. Osterloh & Miss S. Reeves*	2002	Miss E. Clijsters & Miss B. Strycova *Miss A. Baker & Miss A-L. Groenfeld*
1985	Miss L. Field & Miss J. Thompson *Miss E. Reinach & Miss J. A. Richardson*	1991	Miss C. Barclay & Miss L. Zaltz *Miss J. Limmer & Miss A. Woolcock*	1997	Miss C. Black & Miss I. Selyutina *Miss M. Matevzic & Miss K. Srebotnik*	2003	Miss A. Kleybanova and Miss S. Mirza *Miss K. Bohmova and Miss M. Krajicek*
1986	Miss M. Jaggard and Miss L. O'Neill *Miss L. Meskhi & Miss N. M. Zvereva*	1992	Miss M. Avotins & Miss L. McShea *Miss P. Nelson & Miss J. Steven*	1998	Miss E. Dyrberg & Miss J. Kostanic *Miss P. Rampre & Miss I. Tulyaganova*	2004	Miss V. Azarenka and Miss V. Havartsova *Miss M. Erakovic and Miss M. Niculescu*
1987	Miss N. Medvedeva & Miss N.M. Zvereva *Miss I. S. Kim & Miss P. M. Moreno*	1993	Miss L. Courtois & Miss N. Feber *Miss H. Mochizuki & Miss Y. Yoshida*	1999	Miss D. Bedanova & Miss M.E. Salerni *Miss T. Perebiynis & Miss I. Tulyaganova*		